Spiritual Cleansing

Soul Cleansing Secrets No One Talks About & How To Cleanse Negative Energy From Your House In 7 Days (Positive Energy For Home)

Angela Grace

this book.

By reading this document, the reader agrees that under no circumstances is the author responsible for any losses, direct or indirect, that are incurred as a result of the use of the information contained within this document, including, but not limited to, errors, omissions, or inaccuracies.

Table of Contents

Download the 13 Hr + Long Audiobook 'How To Improve Energy Levels: Reiki Made Easy, Energy Healing Made Easy, Protect Your Energy, & Crystals Made Easy' For FREE!

If you love listening to audio books on-the-go, I have great news for you. You can download the audio book version of *'How To Improve Energy Levels'* for **FREE** just by signing up for a **FREE** 30-day audible trial! See below for more details!

Audible trial benefits

As an audible customer, you'll receive the below benefits with you 30-day free trial:

- Free audible copy of this book

- After the trial, you will get 1 credit each month to use on any audiobook

- Your credits automatically roll over to the next month if you don't use them

- Choose from over 400,000 titles

- Listen anywhere with the audible app across multiple devices

- Make easy, no hassle exchanges of any audiobook you don't love

- Keep your audiobooks forever, even if you cancel your membership
- And much more

Click the links below to get started:

Go here for AUDIBLE US: bit.ly/howtoimproveenergy

Go here for AUDIBLE UK: bit.ly/howtoimproveenergyuk

Get Your *BONUS* FREE Manifesting Secret Formula Toolkit!

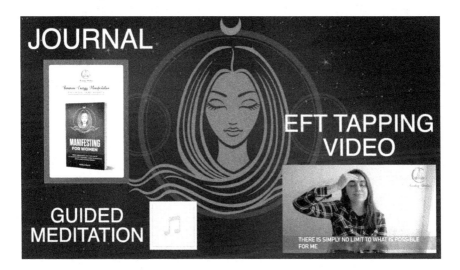

Are you DONE with settling for a mediocre life, wasting precious time, & ready to live your wildest fantasies?

- Hack your brain, boost performance, & release blocks holding you back from greatness

- Awaken this amazing energy to supercharge your manifestations

- Stop wasting what little precious time you have on ineffective methods

Manifesting Secret Formula Toolkit Includes:

1. **Supercharged Manifestation EFT Tapping Video** Download To Banish Limiting Beliefs & Propel You Toward Your Dream Life! (Infused with 432 Hz Frequency)

2. **Secret Formula Journal!** Daily manifestation Ritual Done For You, Simply Rinse & Repeat At Home! (You Can Print This Out, Stick On Your Wall, & Cross Off The Days You Complete The Ritual)

3. **Powerful 10 Minute 'Shifting Your reality' Guided Meditation** MP3 Download (Infused with 528 Hz Frequency)

4. ***BONUS*** LOA boosting 10 Minute 'Feminine Energy Awakening' Guided Meditation MP3 Download

Click Here to Get Your *BONUS* FREE Manifesting Secret Formula Toolkit!:

bit.ly/manifestingforwomen

Please Leave a Review on Amazon

From the bottom of my heart, thank you for reading my book. I truly hope that it helps you on your spiritual journey and to live a more empowered and happy life. If it does help you, then I'd like to ask you for a favor. Would you be kind enough to leave an honest review for this book on Amazon? It'd be greatly appreciated and will likely impact the lives of other spiritual seekers across the globe, giving them hope and power. I read **every** review I receive and they help me to become the best writer and spiritual teacher that I can be.

Thank you and good luck!

Angela Grace

Why not join our Facebook community and discuss your spiritual path with like-minded seekers?

We would love to hear from you!

Click here to join the 'Ascending Vibrations' community:

bit.ly/ascendingvibrations

Introduction

Do you want to cleanse your home and your soul from any negative energy, lifting your spirit and rejuvenating your senses? It can be hard resorting to your home as a safe haven, only to experience energy drainage and constant agony. You deserve to purify the atmosphere, allowing yourself to feel awesome all the time in an inspiring, welcoming environment. There is no place for clogged energy, negative spirits and clutter.

In this book, you will find out how to get rid of the evil eye and lift any curses or hex you have been the victim to. Unfortunately, there are a lot of forces out there wishing to do you harm. You should not let them; instead, you need to build a force field of defense around you, so that you are immune to such threats. There are easy to follow instructions, rituals and routines that you can do, so as to enhance your ability to steer clear from negative entities, earthbound spirits and ghosts.

Whether you have just moved into a new house and want to dispose of the energy from the previous tenant, or you want to start fresh, I will show you the way to achieve your goals. I will guide you step by step towards fully comprehending what you are up against. Only by knowing who the enemy is can you live up to the challenge and face them. What does a curse feel like? How can you tell that you have been the victim of the evil eye? Why do people feel jealous of you and how can you armor yourself?

You will learn more about the aura and its distinct, colorful layers. This is one of the major means of protection for you. The aura has been scientifically proven to exist, as part of your entity. In fact, it surrounds you with a powerful source of energy. In this book, you will see how to elevate your electromagnetic field and attract happiness and prosperity, rather than feelings of sadness and despair. You will be able to open your spirit channels and expand your aura, absorbing negative energy and avoiding psychic vampires and other entities distracting you from your higher purpose in life.

More than that, you are going to learn how to protect your home from any negative energy. There are hostile entities, negative energies, uninvited guests, ghosts and even extraterrestrial implants that you should encounter. This is of paramount importance, as you are meant to feel safe and comfortable within your personal space. When someone compromises that feeling of security, your entire world crumbles down. By using simple ingredients and effective techniques you can use at home, you can suck out all bad energy and create an uplifting environment, where you can be happy and thrive.

Get in touch with your past lives, as they can be of paramount importance to you. By connecting with them and accepting them without judgment, you can do something that most people would never have the chance to do. These past lives are part of who you are, but they do not define you completely. If you have suffered from a trauma in a past life, you can travel back in time and learn more details about it. In this way, you will be able to come to terms with the reality and resolve that endless conundrum you have been dealing with. Instead of swirling in the same vortex again and again, you can sigh with relief and get ready to move on with your current life. On the contrary, you will realize that you can change your course and reach higher levels of divinity in this life.

This book will also help you make the most of your inner energy levels. Cleanse your chakras, ensuring that your energy flows undisrupted. You do not want to see any clogged energy, as this would mean that there is something wrong with you and your body. Make use of modern techniques that can energize your body, enabling you to vibrate at a higher frequency that promotes positive feelings. Benefit from guided meditations that target these specific aspects of your being. Get accustomed to techniques such as TRE, EFT tapping and Qi Jong to promote your well-being.

Finally, get to cleanse your home from bad vibes in just 7 days. A week is more than enough for you to change your life. You will have the opportunity to cleanse your personal space and keep all those dangerous, negative entities out of reach. It doesn't take a lot of time to get these results, either. By using the power of archangels, your guardian angels and your spiritual guides, banish any negative spirit or entity, along with stagnant energy that has been dragging you down. You deserve so much more than that!

My Own Journey

Let me tell you a few things about me and how I came to be involved in spirituality. In my life, I have always been curious to explore the unknown. As a child, I used to ask a lot of questions and delve deeper to get answers that made me feel safe. Growing up in an amazingly loving environment, I was blessed to experience happiness and creativity, hope and optimism for the future. My world was ready to be unfolded before my eyes, opening up a wealth of opportunities.

When I moved out and got into an apartment far from the place I had been raised, all that was suddenly gone. My world lacked balance and I blamed myself for that. I thought I was responsible for all the turbulence I experienced. Every time I walked into my home, the very moment I got through the threshold, I felt exhausted. It seemed as if my inner spirit had abandoned me. No longer did I have the will to create, to wonder, to investigate and expand my horizons. All I wanted was to curl up on the sofa and watch TV until I fell asleep.

However, I could not even find peace and rest during sleep. It was a never-ending nightmare for me. Sometimes I would feel lethargic, but would not fall asleep until early morning. And even when I did, I would wake up feeling equally drained of energy. Have you ever been in a situation, when you know you want something and still can never catch a break and actually get it? I was in a pitfall and I did not know how to get out of this mess. Everything was put on hold, as I could not perform my best. In fact, fear crept inside me and made me worry about what my life was going to be like.

On a bright note, I discovered crystals, energy healing, & spirituality after being introduced to healing crystals by my friend Linda. She was one of the first persons to inspire me towards following that path into enlightenment. I was amazed at the things I heard from her. She spoke about negative spirits and entities from the past that can be trapped within a space on earth, tormenting those around them. She explained to me the importance of spiritual cleansing and self-healing processes. At first, I have to admit that I was a bit skeptical about all that. My mind resisted the thought of someone else being responsible for my emotional and physical ordeal. However, as soon as my mind opened to that possibility and I performed a deep cleanse of my home and body, I was stunned by the results.

Having experienced such great improvement in the way I felt, I was convinced that I was hexed and my home was dominated by negative energy. After getting rid of those entities that undermined my happiness, everything changed. I could now fall asleep peacefully and sleep through the night. I felt filled with energy in the morning, opening the blinds to let the sunlight bathe my apartment. It felt like I finally woke up from a nightmare and I could continue on my path to reach my goals. Once I stumbled upon the magic of soul cleansing and cleansing negative energy from home, it affected my own life and allowed me to thrive. My journey has brought me here, eager to pass on my knowledge to those around me and hopefully motivate them to change their life.

I have written several other books in this niche, all of which opt to give you a new perspective, an innovative look at spirituality. *"Energy Healing Made Easy," "Protect Your Energy," "Crystals Made Easy," "Feminine Energy Awakening," "Manifesting for Women"* and "Reiki Made Easy" are all parts of the same journey. They motivate you to align with your energy, reach out to your divine self and discover the mysteries of the universe. You have the power to do that and I have been blessed to know how to help you succeed.

Join Spiritual Cleansing

Spiritual cleansing can transform your life forever, as long as you have faith. You do not have to feel oppressed, settling for negative thoughts and emotions. It is in your hands to elevate your vibrational frequencies, discarding anything that has been dragging you in the mud. You need to spread your wings and fly away, in searches of new uncharted lands. Why would you ever want to take things for granted, surrounded by disbelief and continuous compromise?

Once you purify your psyche, your spirit and your home, you will instantly find that precious relief you have been searching for. It will open a new world of possibilities for you, as you will no longer be kept down by negative entities that wish nothing but to harm you. As long as you adhere to the easy and simple guidelines I have laid out for you in this book, you can be sure that your world will be an entirely different place from now on.

Do not let others suck your energy and withhold you from accomplishing your higher intentions in life. You have been destined for great things. Therefore, you should not be consumed in a never-ending cycle of negativity. This weakens you over time, preventing you from enjoying life to the fullest. You cannot have that. Not when there are abundant benefits to discovering the secrets of spirituality.

I have gathered these secrets in this book for you to apply in your life right away. Do not waste any more time. Let the power of the divine bless you from within, shedding light on your darkest fears and casting away negative energy. Join me in this endeavor to transform your existence, expand your perspective of life and actually be happy. Be present in the moment, appreciate who you are and what you have been blessed with in life, finally getting what you deserve.

Keep reading this book if you are intrigued about the endless possibilities of your mind, your body and soul. Start studying and prepare yourself to get dazzled. There are a lot of wonderful things that you can do, rather than sit idle and expect negative spirits and malevolent presences to leave on their own. You have the power to make them go, whether they want to or not. It is all in your hands, as long as you know which buttons to push. With just a few tweaks here and there, you will see your whole life change course. Good luck and stay blessed!

Chapter 1: You, Your Family, Your Pets, Your Food, the Trees Outside and Everything Else Are All Universal Energy

Look around you. What do you see? The leaves on the trees, the gentle breeze and the smells of blooming flowers, the sun rays bathing the houses, the birds chirping blissfully in the background. This is a majestic landscape out in the countryside. Not all of us have been blessed with such scenery in our daily routine. So maybe what you see is bustling streets, cars stuck in traffic, people rushing to finish their work for the day, neon lights. Even though these are entirely different surroundings, they do have something in common. They are ultimately Geometry in perfect alignment.

According to Greek mythology, Atlas was given the exhausting task to hold the globe in his hands. This maintained universal balance, although it was obviously excruciating for the Greek tragic hero. Many poets have praised Atlas for his perseverance and selflessness. If he let go of the celestial spheres, the world would collapse in a matter of seconds. Everything would turn into dust, even the slightest wrong move of a single person. (Wikipedia Contributors, 2019) This myth has obviously been discredited by modern Science. However, it teaches us that balance is much more difficult to achieve than we think.

The universe has been created in absolute harmony and you are a part of this global masterpiece. But what does this mean? How can the world function properly, rather than fall into chaos? The answer lies within the concept of universal energy. There is energy hidden within every single one of us. Energy dictates our movements and ensures harmony all around. Otherwise, it would be impossible to coordinate our entities and avoid continuous crashes.

What power guides the universe? There is an exciting theory that explains it quite accurately. Based on the Constructal theory, the design of the atom and the cosmos are the same in their very core. They are almost identical, just like replicas. The way a molecule emits energy and vibrates is the same as that of the cosmos. Energy is infinite and flows through every being, every part of the universe, everything we perceive through our senses. What changes is the complexity of the design. Smaller structures require simpler architecture, which is perfectly understandable (Bejan & Lorente, 2010).

We live in a pulsing and vibrating universe of advanced harmony. You are vibrating also, as part of the universe. Everything in the universe is energy, but it is spread on different levels. Just take a moment and imagine the vast power of energy in a single atom. There is a massive energy that flows through you, through me and through everything in between. A single molecule could as well light up a whole town for a day, should its energy be concentrated and repurposed.

If the tiniest living organism contains an immense quantity of energy, then what happens with individuals? What happens with groups of people, communities, entire cities or countries or even continents? How much energy does that amount to? The numbers are jaw-dropping. Although it is impossible to quantify such energies, it is fair to conclude that there is inexhaustible energy all around us.

If you are determined to clear negative energy and create a positive self and home environment, it is imperative that you understand how the universe works. Otherwise, you will not be able to succeed in your endeavor. Therefore, it is crucial to comprehend that you are not isolated, operating independently from anything around you. Instead, you are swimming in an ocean of energy. This energy is inexhaustible.

The Universal Energy of Frequency and Vibration

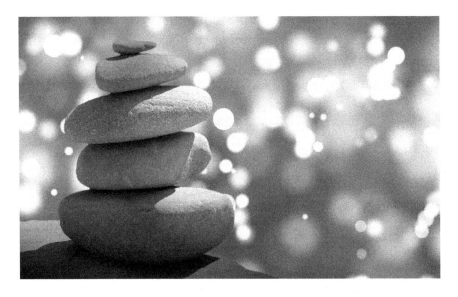

"The field is the sole governing agency of the particle," as Albert Einstein has described most eloquently. An invisible plexus of energy is everywhere, creating matter and preserving it. All the cells and molecules are dictated by the

same principles and governed by the same power, forming each creature and sustaining it for life (freeAgent42, 2018).

Quantum Physics has attempted to explain the principles governing the universe. Subatomic particles adhere to specific rules, which define the world around us. Between the nucleus of every atom and the electrons surrounding it, there is electromagnetic energy. This is invaluable, as it shows there is a continuous flow of energy surrounding everything in the world. Rather than staying still and concrete, reality is ever-flowing. Whether we perceive it or not, the universe is constantly changing based on that very energy.

Energy is everywhere, vibrating at a specific speed to influence reality. When we listen to a single sound, our ears translate vibration. The same happens with all our senses. This is the way to perceive the world. Without this movement, we would be unable to comprehend what lies ahead. Reality has been structured through vibrating pulses. Since we are part of existence, we are also frequency generators. We emit energy to the world, influencing it at a distinct level.

What is even more enticing of a thought is the fact that we can change the world, according to our frequency. The Law of Attraction suggests that an individual's inner state affects the surroundings, eventually attracting the things that are manifested through their thoughts and feelings. This is a shocking revelation, as it allows people to transform reality by changing the way they feel (Corbin, n.d.).

The cosmos is within you. You can shape it any way you want it, as long as you modify your inner self accordingly. Do you seek health, prosperity, fame and money in your future? By manifesting them from within, you make sure that you attract them into your life. On the other hand, if you focus on negative emotions, then this is what you are going to attract. It is a natural course of events, which you are responsible for through the Law of Attraction.

This is an amazing feeling, being able to influence the universe through your own power. As soon as you comprehend how it works, you will be able to attract all those wonderful things in life. You will have the opportunity to devote yourself to your true purpose, without the distractions that have been dragging you down all this time. Now you will be free to create, explore, inspire and motivate others to join your path.

You Are Part of the World

The emotional focus of people in a single event could form universal consciousness. This is how powerful vibration is. When a natural disaster occurs, there is a spike in the global energy that resembles the spike following an earthquake. People get emotionally affected when hearing about a negative event and this emotion is manifested through a change in the global energy. We are part of something great, parts of a Whole that lives and breathes in unity.

That being said, it makes sense that all living beings within the universe communicate with each other. You can talk to the spiritual entity of all things, as they can talk to you. This is the concept of universal intelligence. Take for example the work of Japanese researcher Masaru Emoto. He experimented with water, exposing different containers to different emotions and stimuli. The results were amazing.

Water that had been transformed into impressive molecule formations, whereas water subjected to negative stimulants became ugly and disfigured (Pitkanen, 2018).

When energy remains stagnant, things around it start to wither and fall apart. Life is maintained only through vibration. Once the energy is blocked, this vibrational system is disrupted. The outcome is truly heartbreaking. There can be no life without vibration. Your existence depends on the frequency at which you vibrate. You can change that frequency by charging yourself with the power of items, individuals and emotions that emit elevated levels of vibration.

Only through unconditional love can we achieve that connection with the universe and reach harmony. Forging a connection with this universal consciousness is of paramount importance. Although it sounds awesome, there are hurdles getting in the way of making that happen. In a turbulent environment filled with distractions, focusing on one's spiritual self becomes a lot harder.

By accepting that the same energy flows through everything around us, we instantly become stronger. We fully comprehend how the universe works, charging all things with positive energy and enabling them to reach their higher purpose. You are part of the world, hence you should opt at charging your body and your environment as high as possible. In this way, you will get the opportunity to attract positive things in life, through the Law of Attraction.

Connecting to the Universe Checklist

Below, I have created a quick checklist of some of the things you need to consider to draw your conclusion as to whether or not you are connected to the universe. Answer truthfully, as this will affect your further development. There is no reason to blame yourself, if you find out that you are less connected than anticipated. On the contrary, it is great that you have found out soon enough, so that you can align your energy and restore your profound connection with the cosmos.

- What is your relationship with animals? Do you have a pet? Do you love animals and interacting with them?
- Do you enjoy being outdoors? Do you often go on excursions, taking the opportunity to discover true gems of nature?
- Are you drawn to astronomy? Do you spend time looking at the stars in the sky? Do you read about the planets and the moon?
- Do you often find yourself in a "deja vu" state, when you think that you have had the same experience in a different life (or maybe in a parallel universe)?
- Do you recycle? What do you do to help the environment? Are you a volunteer or do you ignore the imminent dangers for the planet and our survival?
- Are you interested in weather forecasts? Are you more focused on the prediction than the actual weather conditions?
- What is your relationship with technology? Have you developed an addiction to electronic devices and the

web, or have you managed to maintain a healthy relationship?

- Do you think it is probable that you have lived different lives in the past, or do you believe that we only live once?
- Do you often resort to medications even for mild discomfort, or do you prefer alternative medicine?
- Do you have any indoor plants? Does your home have a balcony? If so, do you have plants there? Or do you live in a house with a garden?

Remember that there are no right or wrong answers here. This checklist should only be used as a point of reference, in order to realize how attached you are to nature and the cosmos around you. Do you believe that you are connected to the world through a mystical, invisible cord? No matter what your answers have been, it is in your hand to change your attitude towards nature and the world.

Chapter 2: Meet Your Adversaries; the Evil Eye, Negative Energy and Dark Forces

The evil eye, or malevolent gaze, has been widely accepted as a concept ever since antiquity. All over the world, there are many different words describing the very same thing; an individual's envy may interfere with the good fortune of another individual. Many people believe that this is nothing more than superstition. However, it is a matter of causality.

Have you ever found yourself in a position, when someone else has looked at you in contempt? What has that caused you to feel? I am sure this gaze has affected you for a while, or even for an entire day. The art of seduction lies within the power of a single look. People use it to become more attractive, lure, or potentially manipulate others. Through subtle manners of action, a look can get you what you want or distract you from your goals.

When someone is jealous of you, they will most probably react badly even without them knowing. Their gaze might send negative vibes your way, affecting your existence. Envy is a severe negative emotion, preventing an individual from honestly being happy for the blessings of another person. There are people who envy others subconsciously, since they directly compare them to their own life. What they are deprived of, they cannot accept to see in others. This can be a slippery slope, as there will always be something you do not have.

It is important to note that there are various references to the evil eye in spiritual books, as well as the Holy Scriptures. Hence, it should not be considered as a paganist concept that holds no ground. More than that, there are ceremonial rituals in many religions all over the world aiming at removing the evil eye from the person who has become a victim to its overwhelming power (Bledsoe, 2013).

If you are determined to cast away the evil eye, what you need to do first is become aware of its existence. Unless you acknowledge that it is there, you won't be able to fight it off effectively. Imagine you are preparing yourself for a job interview. You are advised to wear a suit, so as to increase the chances of getting the job. Where does the causality lie in this example? You cannot possibly believe that by dressing smart you can impress the HR department. What you can do is become aware of what you are wearing and acting accordingly. Your behavior will in turn reflect your confidence, leading to a significant increase in your chances to succeed.

Wearing a talisman against the evil eye works like that. You become aware of the threat that is related to the malevolent gaze. More than that, you let others know that you are aware of this threat. A person who is about to cast you a curse will think twice upon noticing that piece of jewelry that shields you against such dangers. That being said, a simple amulet may not be enough to keep the evil eye away from you. It is going to help you, though, as part of a holistic approach of identifying the evil eye as a curse and protecting yourself against it.

You need to know your adversaries, before being able to rise to the challenge and confront them. Learn how to spot the warning signs of the evil eye, in order to realize when you need help. See through the curses cast upon you, so that you can act fast and lift them prior to affecting you dearly. Defend yourself, creating a protective wall that does not allow threats to penetrate its interior.

What Does a Curse Feel Like?

Are you wondering if you have become the victim of the evil eye, or another curse or hex? Do you feel like you can never catch a break? Are you constantly miserable, failing in everything you do? Is there an outside force preventing you from reaching out to your dreams? This is no magic, unlike what many people might claim. Someone does not drain you directly of your energy. It doesn't work like that. On the contrary, it is the impact of negative energy cast upon you, making your life more difficult. This is the curse, which can interfere with your well-being and turn your existence into an ordeal.

I know this all goes against what you have been taught in your life so far. You have been used to sending positive energy to others, praying for them and hoping that they are happy, healthy and accomplished. Your sole intention has always been to spark joy in other people's lives. How can another being seek the entire opposite thing for you? Is it true that there are entities out there undermining your well-being?

Curses are real, because you believe in them. Why do people cast curses in the first place? Curses are meant to bring chaos into your life. However, there is a widespread misconception about the way they are cast to someone. You may believe that there is a whole ritual behind curses. There are rituals, as well as prayers to malicious powers. This is a conscious effort to send out negative energy. It happens intentionally and it is meant to harm you. At the same time, though, there are many curses cast unintentionally. Mothers can cast a curse on their children, siblings can cast a curse on one another, even people who are meant to compliment you can do so without them knowing. It is less common than the traditional aspect of the malevolent eye, but it can happen.

Wishing bad things is more common than what you may think. Take a moment and picture a busy street in the middle of the day. You are driving, when another driver starts swearing. They are calling you bad names, simply because they want to drive past you. Just the thought of you standing in the way and distracting them from their goal is enough to curse. That negative energy takes its toll on you, as you are feeling exhausted because of that incident. Well, it is not by chance. The same happens at the supermarket, when people fight over a bottle of milk or the last candy bar by the cashier. They fight over Sports, Politics, current affairs and so much more.

That being said, some people spend their life never worrying about being cursed. They never think twice about it, as this is not something that usually comes up as a topic for discussion. It usually takes a huge shock for someone to start questioning their life. After hitting rock bottom, it is in our nature to contemplate all the things we have done, in a desperate need of answers. What has led us here and what has made us fail? Is it our own incompetence, our lack of determination, or is it something way beyond our grasp? Oddly enough, a curse is the culprit in many cases.

Cords of attachment bind your own negative feelings with those of others. You must be familiar with duality as a concept. Action comes with the respective form of reaction. Since we can send out love, compassion and light, it is only fair that we are able to do the exact opposite. It is within people's powers to send distress, pain and agony to others. Obviously, you need to be aware that by sending specific emotions, you attract them right back to you. So basically, whoever wishes negative things for others usually suffers even more.

When you receive the negative impact of a curse, your body's frequency absorbs it. As a result, your vibrations change radically. They become lower, which in turn leads to creating negative situations and attracting negative emotions—The perfect vicious cycle. Sometimes, earthbound spirits might join this downward spiral. They cling on to you, while having unresolved issues on their own.

Does a curse affect everyone in the same way, or are some people immune to such threats? Why are some people more susceptible to curses? First of all, people who believe in the evil eye and curses are those who get affected the most. However, ignoring the power of curses will not have a direct impact on the victims. They will still be cursed, they will still suffer, but they will most likely not connect the dots to realize what has been the cause of their ordeal.

Furthermore, being in a vulnerable state within your life helps you become more susceptible to curses. If things go really well for you, if you are in a loving relationship, if you get pure satisfaction out of your work and interaction with others and feel complete, then your shield has been lifted. You can keep those threats at bay far more efficiently. On the other hand, when you are feeling down and you are constantly doubting yourself, if you are unhappy in your relationship or feel trapped professionally, then your guard cracks open.

This all boils down to your vibration. When you emit vibration at lower frequencies, you attract negative things. You attract the evil eye and you motivate others to cast a curse on you. In times of big transitions, this phenomenon can become even more intense. These negative entities feed on your fear. When something big happens in your life, even if it is very good for you, it brings out insecurity. Even if you have just been promoted with a significantly big raise in your salary, you still feel afraid of what is going to happen next. This will be interpreted as weakness, attracting negativity.

Cast Curses Away

There are many different techniques out there to help you remove a curse. Whatever you do, you must be really committed to that. Do not let any distractions lead you astray. Then, you should have someone you trust, a friend or a spiritual guide, by your side. This will help you maintain your focus, while increasing your own power to remove negative spirits and curses from your body and home.

First of all, you can take a white, yellow or black candle and hold it in your palms. Look at it carefully, focusing your gaze on its material. While you are doing that, visualize that you are sending all the negative energy from the curse in this candle. Bring out the emotions associated with the curse, including your fear, anxiety and despair. Along with that, recall all the manifestations of this curse, as far as you know of. For instance, has the curse resulted in losing a precious belonging of yours? Has it made you sprain your ankle? After having concentrated for a few minutes, get that candle and let it burn somewhere without distractions and without blowing it out.

Alternatively, you can use the freezer spell. Just keep in mind that this spell is only effective if you know who has cast the curse on you. Write down the name of the person who has cursed you on a piece of paper. Then, take the paper and put it in a mason jar. Fill the jar with water and place it in the freezer. You can also use the person's picture or a personal item of theirs. The concept is quite simple, as through this spell you have the opportunity to freeze the energy of the curse. At the same time, it creates physical distance between this person and yourself.

In order to get rid of a curse, any type of energy healing will help you out. Reiki, aura cleansing and angelic energy will allow you to lift a curse. Nevertheless, you will need someone else to perform that energy healing on you. You have been affected by the curse, therefore you might be blindsided by it and not be able to remove it like you should. Alternatively, you can ask the person who has come to heal your energy to pray for you. In this way, you can join forces and amplify the energy you both generate. You can then remove a curse far more easily than you would by praying on your own. After all, there is strength in others!

Chapter 3: Aura Mastery, What You Need to Know to Manifest a Joyful Existence

The aura is the illuminating electromagnetic energy that surrounds your body. It is like a protective blanket that follows your exact shape, formed to connect you to the world. To describe it more accurately, I would say the aura is egg-shaped and subtly colorful. As you become more aware of its presence, you get to realize how vibration actually works. You fully comprehend the importance of clearing the negative energy and get in touch with your inner balance.

Essentially, the aura is a vibrating electromagnetic field that surrounds all living creatures. There are 7 different aura layers in the energy body, placed one inside the other. Think of an onion's interior. It consists of different layers, which become thicker as you get further away from the core. They transmit information from the body to the direct external environment. Each layer has a different vibration and is directly linked to a distinct chakra energy center. The outer layers are higher in vibration, although each layer has its own role.

Never underestimate the value of a single energy layer. Since they vibrate at their unique frequencies, they are irreplaceable. They blend together in harmony, creating the individual's aura. A healthy body oozes with balanced energy and this can be shown through a rainbow-colored aura, balanced with a variety of chromatic shades and without any distortions. Always keep in mind that the aura is dynamic, meaning that it can change at any time, depending on the way a person is feeling and what they are thinking.

Learning about the essence of the aura is necessary, in order to comprehend the importance of balancing one's energetic fields. Electromagnetic energy is everywhere, affecting even the tiniest molecule in the universe. Energy creates and sustains life, providing an indestructible bond between the physical and the spiritual world. If you are determined to improve your life on all levels, you cannot ignore or underestimate the meaning of energy. Instead, by embracing the aura and enabling yourself to purify its different layers, you will notice a remarkable change in the way you feel.

Later in the book I will show you how to cleanse auras and give step by set instructions, so that you make the most of their amazing potential. Remember that clearing your energy and the negative energy in your home is of the essence for a joyful life. But first of all, after having grasped their meaning and where they come from, it is only fair that we move forward with distinguishing the different layers of auras. In this way, you will have the chance to address any red flags depicted by your aura. Think of them as indicators of your physical and spiritual health.

If you want to see your aura on a piece of paper, then you can search for aura photography. This is a controversial technique, but you can use it to analyze the different colors, shapes and sizes depicted in the photo. Even if you are prepared for what you are about to see, it can still be shocking to observe your electromagnetic field like that. It is even more disturbing, of course, if you find out that your aura is disfigured. This means that you have some sort of energetic imbalance that you need to take care of, in order to restore a healthy and lively aura.

Layers of Aura

As we discussed, there are 7 different layers of the aura, associated with the 7 chakra energy centers within your body. The first 3 aura layers, the ones closest to your physical self, represent the physical plane. The astral body reflects the astral plane, whereas the last 3 aura layers represent the spiritual plane. All those layers work together and aim at providing the precious balance of your entity.

- Etheric body: This is found right after the physical body, extending up to 2 inches in size. It is the layer closest to your physical presence and acts as a mediator that transfers the energies between the aura and the body itself. The etheric body is dense and thick, blue in color, resembling the physical body but still having a higher vibration. If you look carefully, you can see this layer with a naked eye. The etheric body is connected to the root chakra. It offers liveliness and structure, highlighting even slight abnormalities that may develop into disease.
- Emotional body: As its name suggests, this is the aura responsible for the emotional balance of the body. You store the emotional energy there. It is connected with the sacral chakra and it can get various different colors. What is interesting about this layer is the fact that when you get stressed, darker holes seem to appear on its surface. This highlights most eloquently how great the impact of emotional distress can be on your well-being. It is almost as if your aura gets traumatized by negative emotions.
- Mental body: Moving further apart from the physical body, up to 8 inches, we find the mental body. The mental body is associated with the solar plexus

chakra. It is bright yellow in color and it is mostly concentrated around the head and the neck. This happens because it is related to the mental processes, reflecting one's personal power. An individual's attitude is affected by this aura. Self-doubts can be catastrophic for the balance of this layer, which may lead to fogginess, clouded judgment and a lack of mental clarity.

- Astral body: As we are moving further away from the physical body, about twelve inches, this aura shows your ability to love and be loved unconditionally. It is light pink and its health is promoted through healthy, intense relationships. The astral body is linked with the heart chakra, connecting the three inner and outer layers of the aura. Once you reach this layer, you are introduced to the astral plane.

- Etheric double: The etheric double is located after the astral body and reaches 18 inches from your physical body. Its color varies and it is connected with the throat chakra. Basically, it mirrors the etheric body and therefore reflects the aspects of your physical existence. This layer protects everything you hold dear in the world. As a result, negative thinking will lead to imbalances and a lack of confidence. If the imbalance is prolonged, then you are at risk of sickness manifestations.

- Celestial body: This is otherwise known as the hologramatic and is associated with the third eye chakra. It is the aura associated with enlightenment and is responsible for higher intellectual knowledge. You can see it at a distance of up to 24 inches from your physical self, in a dovey white color. Celestial body symbolizes your consciousness and the way you perceive things in reality. It is also where your imagination sparks and your intuition is developed on a more spiritual level. Once you strengthen this layer enough, you can connect with the spiritual world and communicate with your divine self.

- Ketheric template: Extending up to three feet from your physical body, this is the seventh and ultimate layer of your aura. It holds a deep connection with the crown chakra, which allows you to understand everything. You can see it in pure gold color. This layer holds the divine knowledge and promotes universal power and consciousness. All the experiences gained so far are manifested through a thorough understanding of the world. In addition, the ketheric template enables you to reach into your soul and look through your past lives. Negative emotions will lead to doubts about your higher self, your purpose in life and the divine.

These layers of the aura work together, so as to protect you from all harm. They are like a shield, which prevents negative energies and entities from penetrating your defense. If, however, even one of these layers does not function properly, then the whole structure fails to work as it should. This is when you are most vulnerable to those threats. In order to restore the balance, you need to cleanse your aura and at the same time recharge it. In this way, you will ensure that it is always thick enough to protect your body and strong enough to keep any negative energies at bay.

Even though the aura is not made of any material, you can in fact observe it. You just need to look closely. You can also touch it and comprehend its presence all around you. Of course, you cannot hold it in your hands like you would hold a jacket or a key. Still, it is fascinating to understand electromagnetism on a different level. This is not just Physics, it is every person's reality.

How to See Auras

Auras come in many colors, but the exact colors you see will reveal certain aspects of an individual's true self. As soon as you see the aura's colors, you will be able to draw conclusions as per one's personality and quality. Blue color characterizes an idealist, who adheres to the moral codes and principles. As the color of the heart chakra, green reflects compassion, trust and love. If you are looking for a loyal person by your side, search for a bright green aura. Red is the color of courage, strength and energy. At the same time, however, it displays anger and a deeper will to destroy everything.

A caring person who opts at maintaining peace and harmony in their relationships is characterized by the light pink color of their aura. Yellow color is usually found in teachers and those who wish to pass on their knowledge to others. It is also typical of communication. Orange is the color of creativity and reflects a person's level of independence. If you are searching for spiritual traits, then purple is the color to look for. It is found in psychics and those who communicate with the spiritual world. These people can guide you to your path towards spiritual awareness.

An even deeper connection with spirituality is displayed through a white aura. This is the reflection of a person, who has comprehended their higher self and has flooded the world with enlightenment. White color is that of purity and people with white predominant color manifest cosmic wisdom. Green is the color of healing, peace and harmony. So these are also amazing properties, highlighted in your aura. Of course, as mentioned above, the aura is not static. On the contrary, it moves and changes constantly. Therefore, depending on your specific state at a time, it can show different colors. You should not worry about that, as it is perfectly understandable.

You can see the aura either of yourself, or of another person. In any case, you are going to need a dark background. If you are looking at another person's aura, you should allow a couple of minutes for them to get relaxed. At the same time, you need to let go of any thoughts and concentrate. Then, you should gaze at the person, but not straight at them. Try looking a little further away from their head. In this way, you maintain your perception of the person's presence, but without looking directly at them and identifying any details of their face, or shape.

It is important that you focus on the area of the head, as this is where you get the strongest energy fields. Be silent during the entire procedure, while you are trying to distinguish even the faintest impressions. In the beginning, you will be able to see a white line shaping the person's aura. This is just the first step. As you continue focusing on the person, you will have the opportunity to discern the dominant colors of their personality. Through practice, you can go further than that and see the entire chromatic spectrum of the aura. For those who have been practicing this for long, it is even possible to do so without a dark background.

In case you wish to see your own aura, you should concentrate on your palm. Use a dark background again, but this time keep your fingers spread apart. Look right between the thumb and the index. Do not look away, as you will lose your focus. After a while, you will start seeing that white glow shaped right adjacent to your palm. It will be as if you have dipped your hand in that shimmering light. The more you concentrate, the more you will be able to discern your aura. It takes practice and an open mind, so do not get discouraged.

Chapter 4: Supercharging Your Vibration, Quieting the Mind, & Towering above Negative Forces

If you take a moment and think about it, there is a whole lot of empty space within an atom. This is where vibrations take place, shaping the world all around us. Without vibration, there could be no life. By raising your vibration to the maximum levels, you will achieve the highest level of aliveness in yourself. A heightened vibration can transmute the energy in yourself and your home. So how can you manage all that? Is it 100% in your hands, or do you depend on others?

Basically, you need to understand that your feelings and thoughts translate into different vibrations. Low vibrations stem from negative thoughts and emotions, such as anger, sadness, depression, fear and despair. On a brighter note, happiness and optimism, love and affection.... These are all elements that make your vibrations higher. Just to keep a perspective, a healthy human body ranges from 62 to 70 MHz. As soon as your vibrating frequency drops below that point of 62 MHz, your cells begin to mutate. They deform and bring chaos into your life.

Your vibration is not only affected by what you feel. A lot of other factors contribute to that frequency. Imagine the food that you eat. Did you know that they can be destructive to your efforts towards reaching a higher vibration? If you consume a lot of dead foods, such as meat and poultry, you need to be aware that their frequency does not exceed 5 MHz. This is why it is important that you limit your intake of meat and its derivatives. Especially heavily processed food items should be eliminated from your shopping list. You do not benefit nutritionally from such a diet, while your energy is heavily compromised too.

On the other hand, there are foods that actually promote your vibrational frequencies and make you feel better. Raw almonds vibrate at 50 MHz and leafy greens can go as high as 70 MHz. Opt for organic, raw and unprocessed foods and incorporate them into your diet. In this way, you will get all the nutrients your body needs, without having to resort to chemical supplements. Furthermore, your body will thrive by absorbing the nutrients of such pure foods. Digestion is completed much sooner and there is little residue for your organs to filter and process.

Another helpful tip would be to use essential oils. They skyrocket your vibration and enable you to reach new heights. For instance, rose vibrates at a frequency of 320 MHz. This is absolutely amazing. Their aromas can lift your spirit and change your mood, so make use of their great properties. Frankincense, lavender, and chamomile all work wonders for your emotional health. At the same time, you can use crystals to raise the frequency at which you are vibrating. They can help you clear out negative energy and purify your environment. There are many different crystals, focusing on different aspects of your life. So pick the ones you truly need for optimal results.

Moving forward, it is important to express gratitude for your blessings in life. This is another wonderful way to elevate your vibration, as it motivates you to be grateful and satisfied about what you have accomplished in your life. Sometimes we get so consumed by our concerns and the goals that we have set, that we forget to say 'thanks' for the things we already have. Gratitude is closely associated with abundance and this is quite similar to positive thinking. Rather than drown yourself in negative thoughts, fears and anger, concentrate on thoughts that spark joy. Be kind and this will return to you.

Another way to raise your vibration is to spend more time with people that vibrate at elevated levels. You must have noticed that there are certain people, who just walk into a room and the whole place suddenly lights up. These individuals have been blessed with a brighter energy. Through the Law of Attraction, you will receive that positive energy they are emitting by being close to them. In addition, you should spend more time meditating. Through this invaluable experience, you get in touch with your inner self and gather your thoughts on what actually matters. You learn to appreciate the moment, be present and clear out all the noise that might bring you down. More than that, you practice deep breathing. This helps you destress and relax.

Water allows your body to maintain its bodily functions and stay healthy. However, it also enables energy to circulate. By detoxifying your body, you get rid of negative energy and cleanse yourself on various levels. Simply by upping your daily water intake, you will start feeling amazing. Next, work out in a way that makes you happy. Dance, move around and feel the benefits of energy overwhelming you. We have not been designed to sit all day in front of a screen, or lie down on our sofa binging on TV. Bring motion in your life.

Techniques to Raise Your Vibration

Besides changes you can make in your daily routine, like the ones that have been described above, there are also several techniques you can incorporate for optimum results. These techniques will help you reach a higher vibrational frequency, so as to manifest the things you want in life. They will allow you to reach your divine self and clear any negative thoughts.

Flutter Breath Technique

The flutter breath technique is a great option for you to try out, as it enables you to connect to your higher self. You need to sit comfortably, in an erect position. This means that your chakras should be aligned, creating a channel for energy to flow through without obstacles. Then place your palms on top of your thighs, always facing up to receive. Remember to keep the tips of your thumb and index connected, gently touching each other. Keep the other three fingers connected, too. This is important, as you don't want to let the energy go to waste.

Stand in that position and rest. As soon as you feel relaxed, you are ready to move forward with your breathing. Close your eyes and start inhaling and exhaling through the nose as fast as you can. The aim here is to reach four times a second, which might sound impossible. However, through constant practice, you can achieve that. Even though you may feel like you cannot do this anymore, it is essential that you keep on breathing like that for two to three minutes.

After these two or three minutes, you can breathe deeply and gently. Always keep focused on your third eye chakra. This will help you realize your energy. It will be high, but a bit chaotic at first. Continue breathing deeply, in and out. Eventually, you will become aware of the subtle difference of your higher vibration. Through this technique, you can also focus on your manifestations.

Morning Yoga

Yoga is always helpful to introduce you to your spiritual self. Find a cozy place, bathed with sunlight and get your morning Yoga ritual. Get a comfortable seating position, with your spine erect and straightened all the way up to your crown. This helps your energy flow gently. Your palms should be placed on top of your knees. Inhale through the nose, exhale through the mouth. Practice these deep breaths for a while.

After having relaxed adequately, you can place your right palm onto your heart and your left palm onto your stomach. This will enable you to reconnect with your body. Continue breathing deeply. Next, place both your palms in front of your chest, in a prayer position. In this way, you are ready to set your intention for the day. What are you planning to achieve today? What is your goal? Take your hands and place them all the way on top of your head. Join them for a brief moment and then take them down to the ground as you are twisting your body on either side.

At this point, you should be comfortable and relaxed. Next Yoga position: Take your right hand and stretch it above your head, so that it reaches as far left as possible. Your left hand should simply touch the ground. Do the same in the other direction, continuing to breathe deeply. After that, you can take your hands and bend the elbows, touching each other in front of your chest. Open up, getting your hands on either side of your body as if you were opening a window. Close the hands and repeat the same pattern.

Stretch your arms on top of the head, in front of you and at the back. Then you can change your position. Cat-cow pose is perfect for now. So place your knees and palms on the ground. Inhale while getting the cat position, arching the back. Round your back as you are exhaling, for the cow pose. Repeat for a few times and then continue with the downward dog position. Create a triangle with your body, shifting a heel at a time. Next, do the forward fold position. You are free to experiment with different movements, as long as you feel the energy flowing.

In order to relax and get completely grounded, you are greatly advised to wrap up your Yoga ritual with a child's pose. Get your knees touching the ground, as you take your arms and stretch them as far as possible to touch the ground in front of you. Your whole body is relaxed and you concentrate on your breathing. Let go completely and feel yourself melt into the ground below you. Close this session by following the same routine as you did in the beginning. Sit comfortably, get your spine straightened and feel the energy flow through your chakras.

Fire Breath Meditation

By following this technique, you benefit from the massive energy of fire in your life. It is best if you can be outdoors for this meditation, as this will allow you to enjoy nature. In addition, you can get your feet standing on the grass. Grass will enable the energy of nature to run through you. However, even indoors you can do that with great success. Get your socks off and stand comfortably. Stop thinking about anything, since you cannot opt for a higher vibrational frequency if you are distracting your mind.

Calm your mind, so that it remains peaceful. Ground your feet and focus on your breathing. As you are inhaling, do that with your palms facing up in front of your chest, slowly elevating with your inhale. Respectively, as you are exhaling, keep your palms facing down in front of your chest and slowly move them downwards. Keep your eyes closed for a state of deeper relaxation.

So what you do is visualize every breath you take. You breathe in and then you move your breath into your stomach. This is the core of your energy, which will help you disperse that energy all around you. By using your hands, push the energy as you are breathing, so that it reaches your stomach. As you are doing that, you will be feeling a tingling sensation all over your body. It can be your face, your arms, even your feet.

After completing a round of this breathing technique, you might be experiencing dizziness. This is absolutely understandable, as it shows you have accomplished to raise your vibration. Slow your breathing, concentrate on calmness and get back to the initial state you were in. The more you practice this meditation, the more you will be amazed at the impact it has on your physical and spiritual self.

Practice EFT

EFT Tapping is an alternative method of dealing with pain and distress in your body. It resembles acupuncture, since it focused on certain parts of your body that can promote healing from within. According to EFT, the source of disease is nothing more than an imbalance of energy within your body. As a result, you should restore that balance to improve your health.

Of course, there are specific parts of the body based on the meridian points that you should focus on. These parts include your chin and upper lip, the area below your eyes, the eyebrows, under your armpits and your chest. These very parts are pathways that release any energy blockages, allowing the energy to flow through your body without any obstacles (Anthony, 2017).

If you want to try this out, you can start with a simple EFT tapping session. Take your one palm and begin tapping on the external part of your other palm. I know that you will be feeling your vibration rising by the second, which is great. As you are doing that, repeat positive affirmations. For instance, you can say *"I choose to raise my vibration," "It is my choice to feel good," "I am ready to raise my vibrational frequency,"* or similar statements that complete the effectiveness of EFT tapping.

Then, continue tapping your forehead and the area on the side of your eye. This is going to be extremely rejuvenating. You can tap right between your eyebrows, where your third eye lies, under the eyebrows, right below your nose and on your chin. Keep on saying all those wonderful things you wish to achieve through your tapping session. Be focused and detailed, as you will be manifesting your intentions. The more focused and detailed you are, the better the results. Do not forget to tap the area on top of your head, as well as your neck, your chest and armpits. This will help your energy flow, releasing any barrier. Just a few minutes every day will make a difference.

Absorbing Negative Energy

Apart from the techniques that are meant to elevate your vibrational frequency, you should also focus on how to absorb any negative energy or stress from your aura. It goes without even saying that there is negative energy flowing around, blocking your growth, joy and prosperity. How can you deal with that? Do you just settle for the fact that there is good and bad in the world?

It is in your hands to shelter your home and clear any negative energy that has been piling up all this time. One great way to do so is by casting a saltwater spell. What you need is any kind of salt, along with a jar. Pour ¼ cup of salt into the jar and then take warm water and pour it right in for the salt to melt. As you are doing that, repeat your intention: *"I am doing this saltwater to clear out any negative energy from my home."* Take a spoon and stir well, so that the salt is completely dissolved.

When the water becomes transparent, it is ready. Of course, you need to have some label to put on the jar. Write down the date, so that you can keep track of your progress. Along with the date, you can also write down the purpose of your spell. Repeat your intentions throughout the process and be as specific as possible. *"I am making this saltwater to clear negativity from within my home, cast away all the fear that is surrounding us and be free,"* or something like that.

After a month, you will get the results from this spell. Any negative energy will have displayed as a band around the jar. The water will have evaporated and crystals will have been formed in the bottom. In this way, any negativity is absorbed by this spell, rather than disperse in your home. It is interesting to keep track of the formation of the crystals, in comparison with the way you feel. For instance, if you have just had a fight in your home, check out the jar the next day. You will be surprised by what you see.

Chapter 5: Casting Your Impenetrable Force Field of Defense

Protecting your energy is of the utmost importance, because otherwise your whole life will lack balance. You are surrounded by an electromagnetic field, which determines every aspect of your being. However, there are several threats omnipresent that require your utmost attention. Even when you least expect it, you can be attacked by those who wish to undermine you. Never should you let your guard down, unless you want to take that risk of having your energy compromised.

When you fall asleep, your consciousness slowly drifts away. This makes way for those who wish to harm you. The results can be disastrous, including restless sleep, bad dreams, experiencing collective fears, lack of rest and so many other negative things. If you are determined to safeguard your energy, you should do that 24/7. Sleeping is not an exception to that. So it is imperative that you plan your strategy holistically, leaving nothing uncovered.

One of the best methods to create an impenetrable force field of defense around you is to use psychic protection with gemstones, crystals and amulets. There are items that have so great powers, being able to absorb any negative vibe and protect you and your home. In addition, quite a few different techniques are available for you to enhance your aura and expand it even further. There are specific meditations, mantras, visualizations and rituals that aim at making you stronger, keeping you protected at all times.

At nighttime, prepare for a restful sleep. You can wear a moonstone necklace to keep you protected. Clear the energy within your bedroom often, never allowing stagnant energy to mess with your inner balance. Complete the day with positive affirmation, setting your intentions for a peaceful, serene night ahead. Use essential oils that can be soothing and allow you to calm down and get ready for bed.

Finally, learn how you can connect with the archangels' energy to cast protection over you. Archangels such as Michael and Uriel are ideal in your endeavors. Michael is your ally in battle, so you should call on him when you are in need to fight. Uriel will protect your spiritual self, safeguarding your divine insights and inspiration. Even though the archangels are always watching over you, protecting you from above, you can always seek help from them to ensure your protection is indeed bulletproof.

Aura Field Expansion Technique

By learning how to expand your aura, you master the art of protecting yourself from any negativity. You need to find out how you can create a powerful energy field, which is going to protect you against negative people and anything that might compromise your well-being. Of course, this energy field is not perpetual. On the contrary, you should make sure to refuel that energy once every month. It is advisable to keep track of your aura field expansion sessions, so that you identify when it is time to strengthen your defense once more.

What you need to do is bend your knees and sit on your calves, with your back straightened. In this way, you will feel the stress and tension on your calves, your thighs and legs. The more you practice this seating position, the more comfortable it is going to feel. Get your palms on your lap, facing downwards. Take a deep breath and repeat until you feel relaxed. Allow yourself to relax in this position, balancing out your energies.

Focus on your breathing and make sure that you exhale more forcefully—this is called *"fire breathing."* You should feel yourself breathing out and visualize how your breath expands your aura from within. By doing so, you create your own reality. Slowly but steadily, you will feel your palms generating heat. You will feel your forehead ready to explode with energy.

As you are visualizing this energy, shape it as a protective shield all around you. Let it solidify and keep it even in every part of your body. After completing this process, sit comfortably and realize what has just happened. You will feel your head slightly heavier. There will be an expanded aura all around you, which you will not be able to describe in detail. However, you will feel the difference.

Protecting Yourself from the Evil Eye

The evil eye is very powerful, reflecting the negative energy of a person that is sent out your way. It can be cast on both adults and children. A child that has been suffering from the evil eye will become irritable and will not stop crying. In an adult, symptoms vary greatly and include fever, body aches, headaches and other flu-like signs. An overall feeling that you are unwell and you do not have the power to stop bad things from happening will surround you.

How do you know that you have been the victim of the evil eye? First of all, you will know. Things will start falling apart so quickly, often without any indication of what is about to happen next. You need to make sure that you are protected at all times, because of the severity of this phenomenon. It is much better to be safe, than sorry. Protection is much better than the cure, after all.

Wear your amulets or a talisman representing the evil eye. Be sure to find something that appeals to you, so that you have it always on you. This type of jewelry will absorb the power of the evil eye. After getting in contact with the evil eye, the amulet will break or fall apart. If it falls on the floor, never pick it up. Replace it as soon as possible, as you will most likely suffer from similar attacks in the future.

If you do not know the intention of a person complimenting you about something, analyze their words. If they are wishing you health, happiness, prosperity or good fortune, but they never refer to God blessing you with all that, then you should be vigilant. The best way to protect yourself is by rejecting their energy altogether: *"I reject any negative energy you send to me."*

Finally, a word of caution. Even though you should feel free to do exactly what you want in life, this doesn't mean that you should not be careful. By exposing your happiness and success to the world, you are inviting the evil eye. Unfortunately, evil is not uncommon. Do not expose things that can trigger jealousy, envy and anger to others. Keep those precious experiences to yourself and to those you hold dear to you.

Opening Your Spirit Channels

You know by now how important it is to maintain a healthy energy field within our body and all around us. If you are determined to make the most of your energy, you should open your spirit channels to let it flow through you. The first energy channel is under your feet. Picture it as a thick layer of white light, under your feet and possibly below the surface of the earth. Then, the next energy channel is located around your navel and solar plexus area. Moving forward, the next channel is your heart and above that is your throat. Your third eye is obviously another energy channel within your body. Finally, there is the crown center right on top of your head.

Start by sitting somewhere comfortably, without any distractions. Release the tensions and let go of your thoughts. You need to be present and appreciate the moment. Concentrate on each breath, keeping your body centered and fully relaxed. You should be aware of your presence. When you have established this connection, draw your attention to the first energy channel. Direct this pure white energy towards that center. For even better results, you can chant *'ohm,' 'amen'* or *'ah'* at the same time.

Slowly but steadily, move the energy towards your second energy channel. Focus on that part of your body, between the navel and solar plexus area. The white light has flooded that area. Continue chanting. Feel the vibrations, as a response to the sounds you are making. Visualize the energy like a flower opening up and move the energy to the next energy channel. Watch your heart as it gets filled with that pure light, before transferring the light even higher to your throat. Chant again, as the energy is moving up to the third eye and finally your crown.

By that time, the energy will have flown through you and will be placed right on top of your head. Disperse it into the universe, as you continue feeling relaxed and chanting. Take a deep breath and experience a unique openness. You can repeat this session daily and whenever you wish to increase your awareness of the physical and spiritual self.

Protecting Yourself from Negative Energy

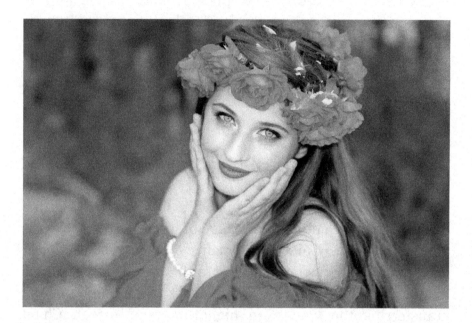

This is a simple exercise to protect you from negative energy, which you can practice before bed. Focus on your heart energy center and take deep breaths. It is best that you place both your palms against your heart, as you are doing it. Fill your stomach when inhaling and exhale deeply. In this way, you will get yourself focused and aligned. Next, imagine a white light of energy all around your body. This is like a force field of pure white energy protecting you. Although it might sound simple, it works really well to create a protective shield for you.

Another thing you need to be aware of is that you can say 'no.' Do not absorb negative energy, do not internalize it, do not get consumed by that. Simply prevent yourself from getting sucked into a vortex of negativity. Allow yourself to let go of things that do not serve your own needs. It is your right to build that wall and prevent others from penetrating it unless you are OK with that. Why would you let these negative thoughts creep into you, draining your energy and making you feel lethargic?

Along with rejecting toxic and negative thoughts, you have the ability to control what each thing means to you. For example, let's say that you have been laid off from work. This is definitely a stress factor, as it represents a huge change in your life. However, you have the chance to think of it as something that opens up a whole new world of possibilities. Maybe you have been stuck in that work far too long. Find the silver lining in this incident, so that you focus on that. It is in your hands to turn even the worst situations into great opportunities for future growth.

Moving on, there is nothing wrong with setting boundaries and creating distance from people around you. It is true that many people are looking for a shoulder to cry on, a person to turn to in times of need. Although this is noble, you cannot be that person 24/7 and expect to thrive in your own life. Since you have a lot more to give, it is only fair that you maintain some boundaries, being strict about what others can get from you. Otherwise, you will always be distracted and eventually lose your own identity.

Confrontations can become a great ally of yours, even if you have grown into avoiding them altogether. Well, I am not saying that you should anticipate arguments. There are times, though, when you need to talk to the person who has been dragging you down and explain to them how you are feeling. Do not be afraid of the repercussions. In fact, this can be part of your exit plan for them. If you are struggling to cope with a person's character, if you are in a toxic relationship at home or at the office, then you must deal with it. Do not shy away from the challenge. Talk it through and either resolve the issue at hand, or get out when you still can.

What about Psychic Vampires?

Psychic vampires are people who suck the energy from other people. They do so, because they do not believe in their own ability to achieve what they want in life. So the only way to get what they desire is to drain it from others. You should be aware that they are weak, helpless and lack a connection with their spiritual self. In fact, what they do to you is a direct consequence of their divine ignorance. Therefore, you should not characterize them as evil.

When you get around such people, you start thinking negative thoughts. As a result, you feel drained of your energy. You cannot cope with the challenges and you deprive yourself of a healthy, happy life. Now, take a moment and think about why these people get into your life in the first place. Maybe you want to be the *"good guy,"* hence you choose to be surrounded by those who are in need of your help. The Law of Attraction works like that. So even though you may have thought of psychic vampires as your exact opposite, they are not.

That being said, you need to steer clear of them. They are deceptive, they do whatever it takes to draw attention to them, they cause guilt and they defend their position against you no matter what. They do not trust anyone and many of them are dissociative. Contrary to common belief, they too feel like they are being drained of their own energy. But most importantly, they will not be saved, regardless of your attempts to save them.

A trap you should not fall for is believing that you need to be protected by them. This will make you feel like a victim. Instead, you need to create a white bubble of light that elevates your vibration, preventing the psychic vampire from affecting you. Since you deprive them of their source of energy, they will most likely leave voluntarily and never look back. Become stronger, so that they do not feed off your weakness.

Crystals and Gemstones for Protection

Crystals are powerful elements that date back to ancient times. Some of them are 1,000 years old and they have been charged with exceptional properties that go far beyond what you could have imagined. There are crystals that have been shaped from minerals, as well as precious stones and gemstones of various shapes and sizes. They come in a multitude of colors and some of them are utterly breathtaking. You can find tiny crystals and gigantic ones that you cannot even grab in your palm.

When it comes to spiritual healing and cleaning of the negative energy floating in a room, crystals are extremely helpful. Due to their composition and thanks to their old age, they are able to absorb a lot of the toxicity that is out there in the world. As a result, they can absorb the negative energy found in your home. No matter if this energy has been caused by entities, by items or by curses, crystals can remove that. It might take time and it may damage the crystals themselves. However, they will do what it takes for you to dispose of the negativity that has been dragging you down in your own personal haven.

- Black tourmaline: It protects your physical body and it is highly detoxifying. Since it works best locally, you are advised to keep it close to you at all times. This crystal has a great energy, which is not compromised through the process of absorbing negative energy from its surroundings. Black tourmaline is considered a stone of protection, purification and cleansing.
- Black obsidian: Technically, black obsidian is not a crystal. It is volcanic glass, created from the hot lava flowing out of the volcano. Can you imagine its power? Having been born through the elements of water, earth and fire, this is a truly powerful item to have for protection. It is incredibly absorbent and protects you from emotional exhaustion. This is called the gemstone of truth, because it clears your thoughts and shows you your strengths.

- Indigo gabbro: Quartz, Feldspar and trace minerals create Indigo Gabbro, this astonishing crystal that is highly programmable and allows you to receive the energy you most need at a time. You get great protection against electromagnetic frequencies, as well as entities. Another wonderful property is that this crystal is able to transmute the energy it absorbs.
- Shungite: there are different types of shungite, all of which are composed of 99% carbon. Fullerenes are elements of carbon, which offer this stone its healing and protective properties. Besides absorbing negative energy, shungite is also able to absorb any detrimental energies found within your aura.
- Amethyst: Amethyst is spiritually uplifting and it is connected to the energy of the violet flame. By having amethyst at home, you help create an environment that is safe and spiritual. It helps you stay protected from spiritual harm and allows you to calm down, relax and destress. This stone absorbs negative energy and transmutes much of it.
- Lapis lazuli: Lapis lazuli is another wonderful stone, protective on a psychic level. If you are even suspicious of having been targeted by black magic, this is a powerful item to hold on to. It also promotes charity of mind, which is invaluable in cases of psychic attacks and negative thoughts sent your way.
- Smoky quartz: This crystal is extremely protective against electromagnetic frequencies, entities and curses. It is highly absorbent and it is quite wide in the range of protection. When you are having trouble, or you find yourself in a painful situation, smoky quartz will help you recover.

- Pink halo: This is also known as Himalayan salt. It is an extremely powerful crystal, used for protection within your home and around it. As it purifies your environment and clears it from negativity, it can also be a great addition to your working environment.

As you can see, these powerful items can absorb negative energy and protect you from it. Your home is a better and safer place, because of them. However, over time they become less effective. This makes sense, as they absorb anything toxic. So you need to make sure that you clean them regularly, restoring their initial composition. You can cleanse crystals and gemstones through various techniques.

One of the easiest and most efficient techniques is to clean them with running water. It would be best for you to go outdoors, in search of running water. Still, even at home you can use tap water and let the crystals soak for at least a couple of minutes. Cleaning crystals and gemstones with sea salt is another option. Just add a tablespoon of sea salt to a glass of water. Place your crystals inside and leave them overnight. Of course, you can use dry salt and cover the stones with it. Again, leave overnight for complete cleansing. Finally, you can use a Tibetan singing bowl. If the crystals and gemstones are small enough to fit, then place them inside. Otherwise, you can get the Tibetan singing bowl on top of them to vibrate and cleanse.

When you notice that your stones are fading away, losing their initial power and effectiveness, then it is time to charge them. You can use the different phases of the moon, depending on your intention. For example, the new moon enhances your intention for growth. So clarify your purposes and charge the specific crystals of yours under the moonlight. Alternatively, you can use sunlight. Using eclipse energies is another way for you to charge your crystals, while you can also bury them into the ground for a specific amount of time. All these techniques restore your stones' former properties and allow you to enjoy their full potential.

For programming your stones, you need to hold them in your left hand and bathe yourself in sunlight. You can do that outdoors, or if you stand by a window. Then, you must repeat the following sentence: *"I dedicate this crystal to light and love,"* in order to express your desire to use it for something good. Next, visualize what you want to achieve through the use of the specific crystal. Once you have manifested your desire, say out loud: *"I dedicate this crystal to the purpose of..."* and complete the sentence with what you want. This is it! Your stone has been programmed to help you in your endeavors.

Chapter 6: Beautify Your Home, Beautify Your Existence

Your home is meant to be your shelter. When you walk through the door of your home, you should feel protected, safe and comfortable. This is the one place you control fully, the place where no one judges you. At home, people spend their happiest and most relaxing moments of their life. So what happens when your home is filled with negative energy? Should you just move, or is there a way to get rid of that bad vibe and restore peace and balance?

Sometimes it can be hard even to detect negative energy at home. There are however warning signs that we simply cannot ignore. Toxic relationships bring out negativism in all its glory. When this negative energy circulates in your home, it will attract more negativity. Over time, the negative energy will pile up and you will feel suffocated under all that pressure. Along with that, when family members or flatmates place the blame on each other, this creates an imbalance of huge proportions. Negative energy blocks your view of acknowledging who is to blame, resuming responsibility when necessary.

Other signs of negative energy in your home feature non-stop complaining, as well as heavy criticism. In any way, you can always look at a glass as half-full, or as half-empty. When there is bad energy, you usually opt for the latter. This creates a vicious cycle, which you are struggling to get out of for your own good. Last but not least, a red flag about negative energy at home is clutter. When your home is packed with unnecessary belongings, along with countless piles of documents, unwanted things that you just can't decide to let go of, it makes sense the energy flow is disrupted.

You need to create a positive, high vibration environment. As a result, you will enjoy spending your time at home, whether with the people you love or alone. Beautify your home, in order to beautify your existence. In fact, archangels like Metatron and Uriel can beautify your home. Metatron assists you in clearing any blockage or negativity from your body or from your personal space. Uriel is the archangel of inspiration and ideas.

There are multiple different techniques enabling you to call on the archangels. You can use meditation, setting your intention to call on the archangel for protection. Focus on your breathing, by calming down your mind and directing your desire to connect with the archangel on a deeper level. Alternatively, you can use exercises, mantras and affirmations. When succeeding in establishing your connection to the divine, the archangel will activate your *"Ascension Pillar of Light."*

How to Detect and Clear Negative Energy

As discussed earlier, there are several warning signs that should tip you off about the presence of negative energy within your home. Nevertheless, if you are looking for some tangible evidence, then you can experiment with some common ingredients you can find in the kitchen. Through these simple experiments, you will see remarkable results that allow you to understand where there are blockages of energy.

The first thing you can do is get fresh lemons and place them in every room. Make sure that they are in plain view and leave them for a couple of days. After that, go back and check their exterior. What does it look like? If your home is free of negative energy, then you will notice that the lemon has not changed at all. In fact, you can rest assured that it will ripen naturally, after a long time has passed.

On the other hand, negative energy can be manifested through black dots or shades on the external surface of the lemon. The lemon will be withered or maybe it will have grown green. In severe cases, it may also be disfigured. If you notice these changes, then you know you should purify the specific room where you have placed the lemon. Otherwise, the negative energy will continue on poisoning the rest of the house.

Another option for you to consider is using a glass of plain water, along with a tablespoon of sea salt and a dash of white vinegar. This mixture is transparent. You should place the glass in a room and leave it for a few days, even simply overnight. If the water remains transparent, then your room has no negative energy. However, if there are stains or if the water has changed color, then you need to focus on clearing negative energy right away.

The Power of Smudging

Burning sage is also known as smudging. This is a powerful technique, which was introduced to the world in ancient times, from indigenous populations that connected to their divine self through specific ceremonial rituals. It has become very popular all over the world, thanks to its amazing benefits in purifying negative energy. Therefore, you can use different varieties of sage bundles available to buy quite easily.

White sage has been considered one of the best qualities for cleansing negative energy. However, in several parts of the world it has almost been extinct. Even if you cannot find white sage, you can use any type and get the same purifying results. It doesn't matter what variety you choose to use for your smudging ritual, as much as how you perform it and how meticulous you are while purifying the place.

What you need to proceed with smudging is a lighter or matches, a heat-proof bowl and a sage bundle. Place the bowl on a steady surface and light the sage bundle. As soon as it starts smoking, you can purify yourself first from toes to head. After doing that, you should go to every room clockwise and let the smoke purify the air. Let it burn out and enjoy a clean, negative-free energy in your space.

It is important to note that you need to blow the sage smoke everywhere, even in the drawers and the closets. This is where your clothes are stored. Even if you are worried that they will smell like sage, you need to remember that you are wearing them all the time. As a result, they have accumulated all the negative energy from people who are looking at you with malicious intent, people who are envious of your success, even complete strangers.

Make Your Own DIY Spray to Remove Negative Energy

Wouldn't it be great if you could make your own liquid to protect yourself from negative energy? Indeed, you could even use it to purify the negativity from within your home, at the office and any other place. Well, the truth is that there are quite a few recipes available for you to experiment with, in order to create something powerful, without any difficulty. This is a simple DIY recipe that you can make yourself, so as to have a powerful ally in your effort to remove negative energy from your home. It doesn't require any technical knowledge and it can be done pretty fast. Remember that this recipe has no preservatives or chemicals whatsoever, so you need to renew it often. These are the ingredients that you are going to need:

- Rose petals (from 4 roses)
- Sage (10 leaves)
- Water (2 liters)
- A pot to boil the water
- Spray bottles

Bring the water to a boil and then remove from the heat. Next, add the rose petals and sage to the water. Place a lid on top and let it sit, until the water cools down completely. When you remove the lid, you should see the rose petals having turned light pink or white. This is an indication that the water has soaked up all their powerful properties. Use a strainer to remove the roses and sage, so that the water is easy to pour into the spray bottle.

This is an all-natural spray, which you can use wherever you want. In order to prolong its expiration date, you can store it in the fridge. The reason for using the specific ingredients is that both roses and sage hold high vibrational frequencies. Therefore, they are exceptionally effective in clearing out negative energy. At the same time, this spray enhances the vibration of your personal space, lifting your mood and promoting a higher vibration for you to attract.

The water can be charged with the power of mantras, so as to absorb energy and purify the environment. You can choose a mantra to chant, if you want to enhance the effectiveness of the water in your DIY spray. The mantra of Lord Shiva is perfect to clear out negative energy. Otherwise, you can place your fingers within the water and set your intention. Repeat an affirmation like the following, while keeping your fingers submerged into the water: *"I am purifying this water, so as to clear any negative energy."*

If you are determined to make the most of your cleansing spray, then it is also good that you charge it with the power of crystals. Black tourmaline, selenite, moonstone and rose quartz, amethyst and so much more can contribute to the strengthened effectiveness of your liquid defense. Experiment with the crystals and gemstones of your liking, mixing them up with mantras and affirmations for optimal results.

Which Incense to Use for Clearing Negative Energy?

In times of extreme stress, when things are looking tensed at home, it is important to create a friendly, welcoming environment. This is exactly the place where energy flows abundantly, without any obstacles getting in the way and forming stagnant negative energy blockages. Incense can be proven extremely helpful in promoting such a positive transformation in your personal space. You can use them on a daily basis, removing any negative energy from your safe haven.

- Camphor: Camphor is often used when you are sick. Thanks to its intense aroma, it opens up your sinuses and helps you breathe deeply. However, camphor is also great at clearing the air and enabling the energy to flow smoothly. It cleanses space, making the area around you friendly and welcoming. Moreover, camphor is quite healing.
- Benzoin: Benzoin is another amazing incense you can use, in order to purify your home. It features intense vanilla aromas, mixed with a wood-like scent. This can be used to remove any negative entities, alongside bad vibes and negative spirits. Apart from driving away negative forces, benzoin is also beneficial to mental clarity.
- Dragon's blood: Dragon's blood incense greatly resembles a perfume. Not only does it get rid of negative forces within your home, but it also attracts positive energy. So while getting rid of the things you do not want, you can also manifest the things that you desire. In addition to its healing properties and

protective features against negative energy, this is an incense that safeguards love.

- Frankincense: Frankincense is another wonderful incense that you can use, since it offers protection from negative energy and purification. It also enables you to become more spiritually aware, while at the same time it lifts your spirit and improves your mood to a great extent. If you are interested in boosting your clairvoyance and stimulating your intuition, then frankincense can work wonders for you.
- Amber: Amber is an equally powerful incense for you to try out, in order to heal your body and clear out all negativity from your personal space. It also helps you gain mental clarity and releases any negative energy that has been piling up and remaining stagnant for long. Due to the fact that it can directly affect electromagnetic energy, in Greek amber is called electron.
- Rosemary: Rosemary is the perfect incense for you to use, in case you are just moving into a new home. This is the resin of new beginnings. If you want to change an old habit of yours or set out on a new venture, then you need to burn rosemary. At the same time, it purifies the space and provides a welcoming atmosphere.
- Sandalwood: Sandalwood can be used to promote grounding in your home. You need to stay connected to the earth and its power. Along with clearing the room of any negative energy, sandalwood also offers a way to stay connected to the central source of energy.

Of course, you can use any of these three incense options or mix them together. Make sure that you stick to a daily ritual, where you burn incense to purify your home and lift your spirit.

Using Essential Oils to Clear Negative Energy at Home

Aromatherapy is a holistic treatment that uses the extracts of herbs and plants, in order to stimulate positive emotions and promote healing (Camille Noe Pagán, 2018). Essential oils are of paramount importance to aromatherapy, as they offer a wide variety of scents that trigger different results. You can use the essential oils with the help of a diffuser, or you can spray them on their own. You can also apply them to your skin, or use them in a relaxing sea salt bath. When you diffuse essential oils, close the doors and let them run for a few hours. They will cleanse the negative energy from your home and lift your spirit naturally.

Lemongrass is an amazing essential oil that you can use, in order to clear negative energy at home. It disperses negativity, prevents feelings of depression, despair and lethargy. Lemongrass cleanses the space around you and offers great healing properties. More than that, it is interesting to point out that lemongrass essential oil cleanses any blockages from the third eye chakra. By letting go of the stagnant energy, you can move forward with mental clarity. You can combine it with sandalwood, which is the oil of sacred devotion.

Experiment with different essential oils, making sure that you create a majestic, positive atmosphere within your home. Do not underestimate the power of aromas, stimulating your senses and promoting your connection to the divine.

Pour Salt in Your Home

Salt has been part of our life since antiquity. People in ancient times realized the value of this special ingredient, which comes from the sea and accompanies us in everything we do. Its purifying properties are undeniable. Therefore, you can benefit from its powerful properties and safeguard your home.

You should use fine salt for protecting your personal shelter. Start from the main room, getting handfuls of salt and spraying them in every corner. You need to follow a clockwise course while doing so, leaving no corner of the house without salt. Of course, you can sweep the salt after a while.

By doing so, you get rid of the negative energy that has been stagnant within your home. You also purify and protect your personal space, as well as avoid visitors that you do not want. Finally, through this ritual you attract abundance, prosperity and serenity in your home. If you are afraid of the evil eye, then salt along with black pepper mixed together in a bowl can serve as repellent.

You can also wash the objects you feel have been charged with negative energy, using warm water and salt. This will help transmute the negative energy. It is also advisable that you use salt to remove any bad vibes from your body. Just place some salt on your sponge or loofah and rub the skin until you feel relaxed.

As you can see, salt can be used in a wide range of situations. Incorporate it into your daily routine and you will notice its remarkable benefits in your life.

How to Clear Negative Energy in Your Home Quickies

To wrap things up, here's a list with easy-to-follow, fast instructions on how to cleanse negative energy at home:

- Smudge with sage: Light it up and wait for a few seconds, until you start blowing. As you blow, smoke will come off and disperse into the atmosphere. Do that in every room for thorough cleansing.
- Burn sandalwood incense: Follow the same procedure as with the white sage, in a clockwise motion. Sandalwood helps you remain grounded, in addition to its healing and protective use.

- Burn Palo Santo wood: Palo Santo wood has a rich fragrance, a little bit of citrusy and with pine undertones. It is a great way to clear negative energy within your home.
- Use a Tibetan singing bowl or Tingsha bells: In this case, use the powerful sounds of those special items. Go to every room, in all four corners. The results are amazing, as you are aligning the energies and using the sound as a vibrational asset.
- Pink Himalayan salt: Sprinkle pure pink Himalayan salt in the corners of every room, with a focus on those you feel the negative energy piling up. Otherwise, you can place bowls with the salt and leave it there to absorb any negativity.
- Meditation music: Another way to purify your home from negative thoughts and energies is to use meditation music. It is soothing and you can choose the vibrational frequencies of your own liking to maximize the benefits.
- Indian basil: Simply by planting Indian basil at home, you are going to get a boost of positive energy and protection. In general, plants are beneficial in your effort to steer clear from negative entities.
- Declutter: Make sure that you throw away anything you do not really need. Instead of hoarding, choose whatever sparks joy in your life and get rid of the rest. You will feel an immediate sense of relief, as soon as you get rid of the old junk that has been occupying valuable space in your home.
- Tidy up: Along with decluttering, you should tidy up your home and keep it clean. There are dead skin cells all over the place, along with dirt, hair and so many

things that mess with your home's energy. Clean them out!

- Visualize: Visualization is a wonderful ally in your efforts to keep your home protected, away from any negative energy. Get in a meditative state and visualize a white light on top of your home.
- Use crystals: You already know the importance of crystals. Make sure that you place them strategically all around your home, so that they can purify the space and absorb any energy that gets clogged up in the corners.
- Ask your spiritual guides for help: You can ask your spiritual guides to help you clean your home from negative energy. Reach out to your dearly departed and seek their assistance in this noble work.
- Spray with the DIY negative energy remover: Use the DIY solution that has been described above for cleaning your home from any negative energy. If you don't have it at hand, then use rose essential oil, because of its high vibrational frequency.
- Use lemons: Place three lemons into a bowl filled with water and let them sit there. If there is negativity in the room, lemons will absorb it and cleanse the place from bad vibes. At the same time, when you place lemons in a room that has been contaminated with negative energy, the lemons will get disfigured.
- Cinnamon sticks: Cinnamon is a great ingredient, not only for spicing up your food. You can burn a cinnamon stick to remove any negative energy from your home. Otherwise, you can find cinnamon incense and scented candles to buy.

This is it! Keep those ingredients readily available within your home, resorting to them whenever you feel that negative energy is clogged up indoors. You do not have to spend a lot of time preparing rituals and trying in vain. As long as your efforts are targeted and to the point, they will be successful. Experiment with their use, either on their own or in combination with each other. Incorporate these cleansing rituals and you will definitely feel the difference right away!

Chapter 7: The War You Are Destined to Win!

We all come into this world carrying our own baggage, whether we are able to accept that or not. We are all flawed, and somewhere in our family history there is at least one rotten apple that we would like to distance ourselves from. There will be diseases in all of us, hardships and things that we feel we cannot survive. Some of these ordeals might be considered as curses, or evil spirits haunting you non-stop. Some others might say they represent dark psychology, reflecting the ability of a wounded soul to manifest these hardships, as a source of punishment or revenge.

That being said, these bad things do not all stem from some evil cause without further investigation. You should first discover the root cause of your issues, before moving forward with encountering them for good. Remember that faith offers you so much, in terms of emotional balance and stability. It allows you to heal your body and soul, experiencing great comfort and deep psychological recovery. Therefore, you need to maintain your faith throughout your endeavors to remove any types of negative energies or entities.

Even the darkest shadows within yourself can be cast away, if you follow the instructions that you are given and do not forget to protect yourself. It makes sense that all people tend to bury those emotions and experiences that had made them sad in the past. These traumatic experiences must get out in the open, even though they may make us feel uncomfortable. This book is meant to provide a loving approach to dealing with these catastrophic emotions, experiences, traumas.

No matter what has happened in your life, both your current and your past lives, you are destined to win this fight. By learning how to cope with the challenges and go to battle against any negative entity, parasite or attachment, you will have all the tools you need to succeed. It doesn't matter if you have suffered from these negative manifestations all your life, or you just discovered the true meaning behind your unhappiness. Believe in yourself and read along, so as to come up with a strategy you can easily follow at home.

Banish Negative Entities, Parasites, Attachments, Curses and Ill Wishes Forever

There are spirits trapped between two worlds, unable to pass on. These are called earthbound spirits and they might haunt you, messing with the positive energy of your home. What you need to do is to help these spirits to go into the light, clearing your place from their negativity. If you are wondering if you fall into that category of having a spirit trapped in your own shelter, then there are several warning signs to tip you off. For example, you might be seeing windows opening out of the blue and mirrors smashing. You may be hearing noises in empty rooms, taps or lights switching on and off in your absence.

The most powerful tool in your effort to remove these spirits from your home is sage. It is extremely effective, as its smoke is able to eliminate negative energies and pulls them out of your place. It has been scientifically proven that by burning sage around your body, you can kill 94% of airborne bacteria (Collins, 2016). This is a great herb, which purifies the atmosphere and enables you to feel positive about the place you live in. Spiritual-wise, it works wonders and assists you in various ways.

So what you need to do is get a bowl and fill it with sage, after breaking it into small pieces. Be careful not to use sage sticks. Use a lighter or match to set sage on fire, blowing continuously to create smoke. Go back and forth in every room, letting the smoke disperse all around. Do not forget to pass by every corner, the windows and doors. Open the closets and blow the sage smoke, then head to the staircase, the attic, everywhere. When you are done, fill the bowl with cold water and get out of the house, closing all windows and doors. After an hour or two, come back and open every window to let fresh air flood your home. Hopefully, the earthbound spirits will be long gone.

Have you ever suffered from a physical parasite? Maybe you ate something and a parasite has crept inside you, causing side effects. Spiritual attachments are parasites of non-human nature, entities that do not want to leave this space. They might even be extraterrestrial implants. They do not want to proceed to what lies ahead, either because they feel guilty, or because they are afraid. Of course, they may have been atheists who do not believe in a higher power. Therefore, they are stuck here. Unfortunately, you are vulnerable to such entities in a number of different cases. You can be intoxicated, or you may have sexual intercourse with a person who has one of these attachments, or you might be in a truly emotional state.

Crystals can also help you in your endeavors to remove entities and negative energy from your home. An amethyst, a rose quartz, a smoky quartz and others should be placed on the window ledge or at a corner of your room. Clapping is another method that allows you to remove those negative spirits. Just clap your hands in every corner of your home, helping the stagnant energy get unclogged. In addition, you can place sea salt in a bowl and then on top of it you can add a coarse crystal. Let it sit overnight and then clean the crystal with pure water. This will help release the excess negative energy.

Last but not least, you can choose to use a powerful prayer to remove those negative spirits from your home. A prayer is your commune with God, with the higher power. You need to remain in deliverance, in order to communicate with that high power and seek help to get rid of those entities. Call on what you believe, praising the Lord and expressing your gratitude: *"God, you are the beginning and the end, you are the alpha and the omega, you are the omnipresent light. You are my creator. I worship you, I thank you for my life. I pray for you God, all mighty. Please my Lord, raise the spirit of my dear brother and sister. Raise their spirit to another level. I pray that with all my heart."*

In this way, you will find that your genuine communication with the higher power has made these spirits go away. Of course, you can use your own words in your prayers. In fact, you can speak right from your heart. Say what you want to express in your own words, reflecting the way you feel about your creator, the creator of all things.

Past Life Cleansing

We have all lived in the past, but most of us cannot remember. Why does that happen? First of all, it is our limited perspective of a 3-dimensional world that prevents us from seeing the wider picture. Then, it is divine mercy that stops us from remembering everything in detail. After all, it is highly likely that in our past lives we have done some terrible things. So we are armored with a veil of forgetfulness, which lets us start over fresh. Finally, it is our conscience that has encompassed the best of our past lives and guides us to act based on love.

Can someone remember their past lives? Of course they do! It is important to remain calm throughout the process, sitting somewhere comfortable with closed curtains and dimmed lights. Steer clear from any electronic devices, including your phone. Avoid any distractions, hence choose a time of day when you have already relaxed from the echoes of your busy lifestyle. Use white noise or other soothing sounds, waves or waterfalls.

Now lay down with your back, get your arms on both sides and visualize a white light surrounding you. Concentrate on all your body parts, feeling the light protecting them with its pure, powerful presence. Repeat positive affirmations about the white light, such as: *"I am breathing in the powerful energy, I am protected by it."* Imagine your aura changing colors, as it expands.

You are ready to begin your journey. Picture a long corridor, with a door at its end. Observe every detail. Keep this in mind, as you will be able to come back again to do the same journey in the future. When you open the door, experience what you find. Feel the energy, listen to the sounds, notice the smells, the textures, anything you can recall. When you are ready to return, push the door gently. Receive that memory of your past life without judgment. Use it as a reference and be grateful for the experience.

By using your birthday, you can see your soul's characteristics based on your past lives. First remember the number of your birth month. For instance, May is 5. However, if you were born in November, then you will add the digits of 11 and get 2. Remember that number. Then, move forward with the day you were born. Again, if you were born on the 2nd day, you will keep it as is. Otherwise, you will add the numbers to get a single digit. Next, add the sum of the numbers composing the year you were born. For instance, 1966 should be 1+9+6+6=22. Finally, add your birth month, birth day and birth year numbers. If you ended up with anything ranging from 1 to 9, 11 or 22, this is your result.

- #1 Alpha: You are independent, concentrated on your goals and rebellious. You do not feel the need to please others, as you are perfectly fine relying on your own strength.
- #2 Peacemaker: You are part of a team, supportive with ambitions to evolve and expand your knowledge. That being said, you are not at all selfish, but take into consideration the common good.
- #3 Creative: You are an influencer, inspiring others through your positive look at things to follow your lead and become more optimistic in life.
- #4 Practical: You are honest, just and reliable. Your practical spirit helps you in everyday life, as you find solutions to problems and help others see more clearly.
- #5 Free spirit: What drives you is freedom, adventure and the will to explore new uncharted territories. Your mind never ceases to dream big.
- #6 Compassionate: You protect others and love humanity. A compassionate person deeply cares about the world, protecting mankind and caring for the future.
- #7 Truth seeker: In constant pursuit of the mysteries of the world, the truth seeker exposes the lies and focuses on cross-checking evidence.

- #8 Leader: You are successful and you want to drive others to glory. You are always ready to fight for what you believe is right alongside your companions.
- #9 Socially conscious: You are ready to sacrifice yourself for the common good, since it is society that you are interested in protecting more than anything else.
- #11 Karmic master: Artistic, intuitive, with a higher sense of consciousness, the Karmic master develops a keen eye for detail, delving into the mysteries of life.
- #22 Master builder: Strong-minded, you influence others and unite them under a common purpose. You are a divine presence on this earth.

Having lived so many lives, sometimes we drag bad karma that affects us dearly in our current state of life. By clearing your past lives' karma, you get to relieve yourself from all the things that have been keeping you away from your goals. Karma can affect you in many ways. For example, you may be struggling to lose weight in vain. This can be because in your past life you had been starving. As a result, this pattern is affecting your healing and growth in this lifetime.

In order to clear past life karma, we need to be fully committed to our current life goals. We must be mindful of our vibrational frequencies at all times. Where do you consume your energy? Do you make good use of that, pursuing your dreams? Or are your thoughts chaotic, not serving your purpose at all? You need to be strict with yourself, if you want to engage in past life clearing. You have your own life to live right now, rather than contemplating the complexes and problematic situations emerging from the past.

Go against your normal programming. It doesn't matter if you have been taught that as you were growing up. If it's not serving your needs and goals, then you need to reprogram yourself. Consciously choose new thoughts, new beliefs, new feelings of optimism and happiness. Along with that, it is imperative that you express your emotions as soon as you realize them. In this way, you can vent and get it off your system.

The reason for doing that is to allow yourself to grieve. You have never been given this opportunity, so you should embrace it, before getting rid of your prior dysfunctional behavior. EFT tapping can help you out with that, as well as keeping a journal or saying a prayer out loud. Finally, you can do a contract release with the behavior that does not serve you. Visualize cutting the cord of anything you wish to change in your life. Write down this contract or say it out loud.

Chapter 8: Cleanse Your Own Energetic Field to Skyrocket Your Joy

I am sure you are looking forward to cleansing your energetic field. This is essential, if you want to experience a happy and prosperous life. There are energy centers in our body, defining our health and the way we feel. These energy centers are strategically located along our spine, creating a virtual column of energy flow from the ground to the sky above. They reflect the deeper and uninterrupted connection between the earth and the universe. It is eternal and omnipresent. If you want to align fully with the cosmic energy, then you need to make sure you become a vessel of energy yourself.

However, on several occasions this energy flow is disrupted

violently due to various reasons. Sometimes a disease strikes, causing imbalances from within. Stress and anxiety, fear of the unknown, feelings of self-doubt and helplessness only add to this phenomenon of clogged energy centers that do not quite serve their noble purpose. They get cluttered, unable to permit the energy flow that is of the essence for your very existence. It is in your hands to take charge and restore your energetic balance as soon as possible.

In the Orient, energy centers have been named 'chakras.' Below, you will see how to cleanse those chakras and boost their functionality. Each of these energy centers has been focused on a specific organ of the body, which means that even the slightest lack of balance will have a direct effect on your physical health state. It is like a valuable cog in a wheel. Without it, the wheel will not move and this will be disastrous to the entire mechanical structure.

Although typically these are the seven chakras, you should also concentrate on another organ of your body. The thymus gland is located right below your throat chakra, sticking out in the middle of your chest. By activating the thymus, you enhance your immune system and skyrocket your energy. If you want to activate this gland, you need to close your eyes and visualize that it opens up gently and utterly. Imagine a flower blossoming, with each petal slowly opening up and revealing the impressive interior. The flower is pink and it expands through each motion. It becomes wider and goes further with each breath you take.

By default, your thymus gland begins shrinking in size at the age of 16 and it continues shrinking with age (M, 2019). You can reverse that phenomenon with the power of your mind, or at least delay it from happening. By visualizing this expansion of your thymus gland, you will most likely start feeling it vibrating more heavily. It will be pulsing. Over time, this gland will allow you to reach higher levels of divine spirituality. You will be more receptive to initiations, while comprehending your uniqueness and putting it to use.

Now that you have activated your thymus gland, let's move forward with a chakra cleansing session that assists you to flood your body with pure energy. Be meticulous while performing this cleansing, as you will need to get rid of every single hint of negativity from your body.

Chakra Cleansing

As you know, there are seven chakras in your body. These represent your energy centers, where the energy flows smoothly and allows your body to thrive. In order for you to maintain optimal health and balance between the body, the mind and the psyche, you should make sure that your chakras are clean. They should be free from any distractions or clogging that might jeopardize smooth and uninterrupted flow of energy. Therefore, it is important that you proceed with a ritual, allowing these chakras to be kept open at all times. You can do it in the morning or set a reminder on your calendar to perform this ritual weekly.

Starting from the top, we find the Crown chakra. It is located on top of your head and reflects your ability to connect to the spiritual world. Right between your eyebrows, there is the next chakra—the Third Eye chakra. This is directly associated with your intuition and your spiritual powers. Next, there is the Throat chakra. It is responsible for your ability to communicate with others and express yourself.

Your Heart chakra is obviously connected with love, appreciation and affection.

Moving on, we find the Solar Plexus chakra below our chest. This is the chakra related to our sense of self-worth and confidence. Sacral chakra is located below your belly and is connected to your sexuality. It offers you a feeling of abundance and pleasure. Finally, there is the Root chakra. This is where it all starts. This chakra is connected to our grounding experience, representing our foundations in life.

How can you cleanse your chakras? One thing that you should do is get a smoky quartz crystal and hold it in your left hand. This is your receiving hand. Then what you do is place the crystal on each chakra, repeating positive affirmations relevant to the specific energy center.

- Begin with the Crown chakra, placing the crystal on top of your head as you repeat the following: *"I am aware that I receive the wisdom I request always"*
- Continue with the Third Eye chakra, repeating affirmations like this one: *"I understand that my intuition is the way God communicates with me and allows me to see clearly"*
- Then, place the crystal on your neck to cleanse your Throat chakra, repeating: *"I communicate effortlessly and genuinely with everyone around me"*
- Move on to the Heart chakra, keeping your eyes closed and saying the following: *"I am Love, I deserve to love and be loved unconditionally and utterly"*
- When you move further down to your Solar Plexus chakra, you should say affirmations like this one: *"I always have the power and drive to succeed in the goals that I set in life"*

- Now that you have reached the Sacral chakra, you should focus your affirmation on your sexuality: *"I feel desire, pleasure, sexuality and self-confidence"*
- As you have made it to the Root chakra, complete your affirmations like that: *"I am abundant in energy and strength. I express my unique self in the perfect manner"*

Practice Self-Healing through Qi Gong

Qi Gong is an ancient traditional technique from the Orient, combining deep breathing, along with specific movements and meditation for achieving optimal results in your inner balance. Your body has the ability to heal itself from within and Qi Gong opts at promoting such properties. Below, you will find a simple yet highly effective routine to energize your body, cleansing your energetic field and casting away all negativity.

Stand up comfortably and open your hands with bent elbows, just like you would open the window shutters at home. Inhale through the nose. As you exhale through the mouth, curl your back and face towards the ground, with your elbows almost touching each other. In this way, you loosen your spine and create a pillar of energy. Repeat 8 to 10 times and then relax your hands. Now, take your palms facing up and shake your wrists. This exciting movement opens the energy pathways that go all the way to your palms, communicating with your heart meridian. As you are doing that, take deep breaths inhaling from the nose, exhaling from the mouth.

After repeating for a whole minute or two, you will feel a tingling sensation. You are ignited with energy. Next, you need to connect to the earth. Shift your weight towards the heels and experience gravity. Let your body get into full alignment with the gravitational power, so that the earth charges you with its powerful energy. Do not forget to keep your palms facing down. Move them up and down, as you are trying to control that energy. Next, take your right palm and place it in front of your belly facing up, while the left palm is on top and facing down. You should feel the energy between your palms. Slowly move your left palm towards your forehead, so that you create a connection between your mind and the body.

What you do after that is to lower your left palm steadily, in order to reach all your energy centers. You should establish energy connections between your mind and your throat, your heart, your solar plexus and below that until you reach a point where your two palms almost touch each other. Then, rotate your palms and move them further apart and close together. This allows you to control your energy completely. Now that you have charged your hands with this vast amount of energy, you can channel it in the parts of your body you feel most vulnerable. You can channel it to the back of your neck, on your chest or anywhere else you want to soothe.

A Morning Ritual to Cleanse Your Aura

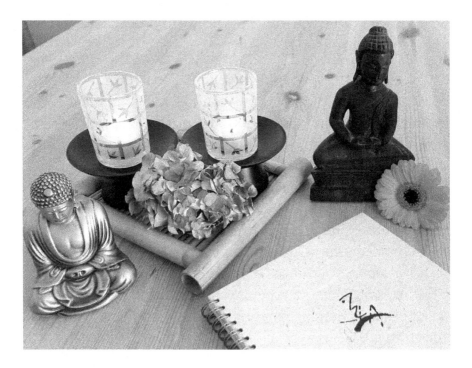

Do you want to start your day energized, ready to take on any challenge that comes your way? Then it is imperative that you clean your aura, so that you restore your body's balance and enjoy its powerful properties. Each morning you should get up and start your day with a tall glass of water, infused with mint leaves. You can also use cucumber slices, fruit or other herbs and spices to mix it up. You will hydrate your body and detoxify from any negativity. Open the windows, so as to flood the room with sunlight and get fresh air. The energy of the sun is impeccable.

Turn on high vibrational music that uplifts your spirit, in order to complement your morning ritual. Take Palo Santo wood, so as to perform a purification of natural cleansing energy. Burn it all around your room, while thinking happy and positive thoughts. As soon as you are down, you will feel so rejuvenated by the exciting aroma it gives off. If you have a salt lamp, then you can turn it on to add to the positive energy within your room.

Then, close your eyes and meditate. Focus on the uplifting spiritual music, the soothing sounds and the intoxicating aromas. Say what you are thankful for in your life. By expressing gratitude, you instantly increase your vibrational frequency. After completing your meditation, it is time to fully cleanse your aura. Get into your shower and let that pure water run all over your body. This is a highly therapeutic experience, allowing you to fully relax. If you have time, taking a bath with Epsom salt is great for the purification of your aura. If you don't, however, you can use dead sea salt. This is a type of salt that has magnesium and a lot of other minerals, benefiting your skin by removing dead cells.

Finish your morning ritual by writing down your positive affirmation in a journal and set out for a new, wonderful day filled with energy!

Energy Cleansing Using Salt

Salt is a mineral and a natural cleanser. People cannot even begin to imagine what their life would be like without the presence of salt. It is always there on our table, when we share our food and we want to make it tasty. It also accompanies us in summer vacations, when we dive into the crystalline waters of the sea and taste its presence on our skins and our lips.

Besides all the important benefits of salt, it is also used for spiritual purposes. It is one of the purest forms of protection for your home, yourself and any other place you wish to safeguard from malicious entities. You can cleanse your home using a homemade solution made with water, baking soda and salt. This will not mess with your home's energy and balance. However, you can use salt directly to eliminate negative energy with its power, through a simple yet effective technique based on Feng Shui.

Get ¾ cup of coarse salt. Then, place 6 I Ching brass coins and place them inside the salt, in a circular shape. After that, get purified water and pour it on top of the salt. You do not need to use a lot of water, just a couple of inches above the salt surface. Place the container somewhere you can easily notice daily. As the days pass by, you will see a large crystal shaping. The water will react with the salt and the brass, creating an impressive crystal that will eventually overflow. According to tradition, this crystal absorbs any negative energy. At the same time, it serves as an excellent visual stimulant of the removal of negativity from your home or yourself.

Egg Healing

Are you experiencing a period of great stress? Are you having nightmares? There are moments when you feel uncertain or you are seeking a deep cleansing in your home. This is when you should turn to the subtle yet powerful properties of the egg. Even if you are skeptical as to whether or not it is going to work, you have nothing to lose. In fact, you will be amazed at the results.

Close your eyes and take deep breaths to relax. Move the egg around the head and rub it over the eyes, behind the ears, at the back of the scalp and down the chin. Then, roll the egg in front of your chest. Swirl it and then move it across each arm, on top of your shoulder and all the way down your palms. Pay close attention to that, as your arms represent an important energy center. As you are passing the egg through each finger, you can hold it within your palm for a few moments. Make sure that you then rub the egg again on your chest, across your angel wings and along your spine.

Move forward with your legs, focusing on your kneecaps, your feet and ankles. Get the egg through each toe and then move it on the soles of the feet. Finally, blow on the egg three times. This will allow you to release your inner tension. During the egg healing ritual, you should be careful not to break the egg. However, you need to be prepared for the fact that the egg can weigh a lot heavier than before, due to the accumulated negative energy. This is why sometimes the egg might even explode.

Another option for you is to use 2 eggs, 1 white candle, a glass of water and some sea salt. First of all, light the white candle and let it burn out on its own. Then, start cleansing your body with the help of the egg. While you are doing this, you should praise the Lord and be thankful for your blessings in life. Ask that all the evil spirits and negativity are absorbed by the egg. Once you are done, you should take the egg and break it inside the glass of water. This will show you what is wrong.

If the yolk gets to the bottom of the glass, then you can sigh with relief. On the other hand, if it stays in the middle or floats on the surface, it means that evil powers are affecting you. If there are a lot of bubbles all around the yolk, then this is the negative energy that makes you feel exhausted and lethargic. In case a figure is displayed on the glass, this is the object of your concern. If there are pointy edges on the surface of the glass-like needles, they represent the negative entities undermining your well-being.

Maybe you see a coat surrounding the egg yolk. This means that there is someone constantly casting negative energy on you. If you notice red or black spots on the yolk, it means that you will encounter disease in your life. A cloudy yolk usually means that you have been the victim of the evil eye. Once you have finished observing the yolk, add sea salt and flush it down the toilet.

Chapter 9: What Is Within, Will Become a Reality on the Outside. Make What Is Within Beautiful

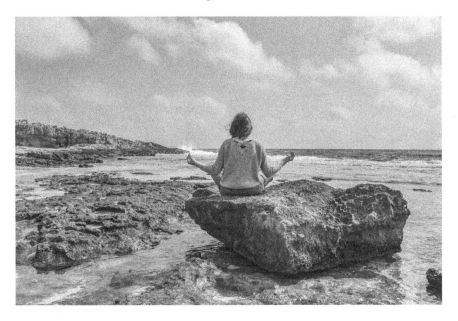

In this section of the book, you are ready to create a new reality from within you, so that you can project it to the world. There are techniques such as EFT tapping, TRE, mantras, meditation and so much more that can help you change your world. You need to disconnect from the ego to clear space, so that negative energy cannot be self-created and pollute the world. Clearing old conditioning that creates negative energy is of paramount importance, if you want to affect the universe in a positive manner.

There is a whole new world before your eyes and you have the power to shape it exactly like you want, instilled with the qualities of your higher self. This world will be loving and accepting. It will not be poisoned by the negativity drawn from selfishness, revenge, envy and jealousy. Instead, it will promote happiness for every being on this earth. You have the power to achieve all that, if you simply manifest what lies within your soul. Make it beautiful, so that the world can see your masterpiece. There are no limitations as to how to shape your reality. Use your imagination and do exactly what you want to do, making sure that the end result is aligned with the cosmos. Find out how to best express yourself, by creating the world around you in a way that makes you happy. This is going to be a fascinating journey.

Use the tools that appeal to you the most, in order to shape your inner self in a way that inspires others to follow your lead. The techniques shared below are self-applied, meaning that you can do them on your own. They are easy to follow, introducing you to different holistic approaches of energy healing. EFT tapping is based on the belief that your energy is soothed and redirected through tapping on acupressure points around your body. These are the meridian points, including many different spots around your head, on your crown, under the armpits, in front of your chest and on the exterior of your palms.

On the other hand, TRE is an easy tool for you to release trapped trauma and energy from within your body. This technique can be used to bring your nervous system back to a steady balance, making space for you to achieve higher vibrational frequencies. You already know how important it can be for you to do so, since all negativity is related to low vibration. By finding a way to get around this, you effectively deal with the phenomenon of attracting negative situations in your life.

EFT Tapping for Clearing Negativity

Have you ever considered making the world a better place through your own actions? EFT tapping can help you with that, energizing those parts of your body that clear negativity and promote happiness. You should take full responsibility for your own joy, with the active contribution of tapping sessions. What you can do is start tapping the external part of your palm, while repeating positive affirmations that cast the world's negativity aside. You can continue tapping several spots on your face (the area under your eyes and on their side, your third eye, your upper lip and chin, your cheekbones and forehead). Below you will find a typical script of clearing negativity within the world:

"Even though there is negativity in the world, I choose to be happy and positive. I accept myself completely, I love and honor myself. Although at times I encounter negativity, I choose not to spread it in the world around me. My choice is to spread happiness instead. I give myself permission to be happy, even though there is evil and negativity in the world. It doesn't affect me. Negative people don't affect me. I will affect them, making them dispose of their own negativity, spreading happiness even wider. Although I get exposed to negative vibes, I choose not to spread them. I clear that out with help from others and continue being happy. I share love, affection, joy and positivity to the world."

There are moments in your life when you feel consumed by energy vampires. EFT tapping can help you deal with this negative experience, if you adjust your script accordingly. As you are moving your fingers through the various meridian points all around your head and body, repeat something like that: "I love and honor myself, even though there are vampires sucking the energy from my body. It is my choice not to let them drain me of my energy, I continue to love and accept myself. Although these people get in the way and prevent me from doing the things I want in my life, I deeply accept and love myself. My intention is to show these energy vampires the way to live without absorbing my energy and bringing me down. I have to put up with them, although they make me feel powerless. My choice is to reclaim my energy and the power that I possess, so as to stop being the victim in this situation."

Another approach would be to use the energy EFT protocol, while invoking angelic power and protection. Your feet should be touching the ground, ensuring that you have higher energy flowing through you. To help you with your session, you can call on the archangels of your choosing. You can call on archangel Michael, archangel Zadkiel and your own guardian angel. Place both your palms in front of your chest, right in the center of your heart. Take deep breaths, so as to maintain your serenity and inner balance.

Once you feel totally relaxed and in sync with your energy, place your right palm on different parts of your head. Start with your Crown chakra and move further down to the forehead, the third eye, the area below your eyes and all the spots you would normally be tapping in a typical EFT session, repeating the following: *"I am releasing negativity now from my body. Thank you angels for enabling me to do that. I don't need to hold on to that toxic energy, so I am letting it go."* After that, touch your left fingers with your right palm and repeat how pure and revitalized this energy feels.

When you finish, you can start over with a different script that enhances your intentions. *"Thank you for the violet flame energy that runs through me. I am grateful for the pure violet energy within me and around me."* To conclude your EFT tapping session, you should place both your palms against your chest. This was your starting position. Close your eyes and visualize the archangels embracing you and offering their protection through the violet flame.

Shamanic tapping is another option for you to clear your mind from all negativity. In this case, again you move your fingers to various parts of your head and body, tapping them gently. You should stand in front of a mirror throughout this session. To elevate your vibration and remove negative thoughts, you can ask for forgiveness about anything bad you have done. There is nothing wrong with assuming responsibility for your actions. In fact, it shows that you understand what is right and wrong, what is good and bad. So you can repeat the following affirmation: *"I am sorry. Please forgive me. I love you."*

After completing this tapping session, you should get your palms in front of your chest and start rubbing them. As you do, begin setting them apart slowly and continue the same motion. In this way, you will be able to generate energy and transfer it from your palms. You should set your palms apart gradually, increasing the distance between them slowly. When they have enough distance apart, you can rotate them so that you form a ball of energy. As soon as the energy is accumulated, you are free to place it on top of your head. It will be like bathing yourself in pure energy. Pull this energy down with both your palms, redirecting it all over your body and repeating how grateful you are for what you have received.

TRE to Release Past Trauma

TRE are exercises used to destress and remove past trauma from patients. They focus on tremors of the muscles, in order to release the tension formulated in the body. Once you put too much pressure on a specific muscle, you get a natural reflex. This is the tremor, which is beneficial to restore the balance from within. As a result, your nervous system calms down. It is a perfectly safe and greatly efficient technique, composing of various innovative exercises that are simple to execute. However, it is advisable that you remain within a controlled environment at all times. Otherwise, your reflexes might cause discomfort.

It can be seen as a combination of yoga, health counseling and massage treatment, when it comes to the provided benefits. If you want to try TRE out to clear out negative energy from your body and surroundings, you need to pick a comfortable place to lay on. You can use a yoga mat or a soft rug. Your intention is to help your body reach a point where it is almost exhausted. To do so, you can lean against a wall with your knees bent. Imagine that you are trying to sit down on a virtual chair right below you. Slide with your back as low as you can, while maintaining strength over your legs. When you feel like you have reached a point where you are trying too much to hold on, then stay in this position. Lift your heels for optimal results.

After a few seconds, you will feel your muscles burn. Stay in the very same position, until you cannot take it anymore. Then, what you do is lift your weight and move your torso a bit higher. It is like you are trying to sit on a slightly taller chair. You do the same, until you feel your legs slightly shaking. This is when you know you have activated your muscles through TRE. If you lay down on the mat, you will experience the tremoring that releases tension and clears the energy.

Another option for you is to fold your body and stretch, trying to reach your toes with your hands. This is equally challenging for most people, as your muscles are under pressure and you are trying to maintain your balance. Alternatively, you can start by laying down on the yoga mat. Your back is on the ground and your legs are bent before you, with your feet touching the ground. What you do is spread your legs and try to make your feet touch one another. It seems like a frog position. Once you are comfortable doing that, you can begin spreading your inner thighs even further and lift your hips.

TRE can assist you in reducing the tension and anxiety, lifting your spirit and creating a welcoming environment. Your vibrational frequencies get higher, thanks to the reflexes that make you shake. In addition, TRE helps you in dealing with chronic pain and promotes emotional resilience.

Instant Aura Cleansing

Your aura is meant to protect you at all times. Nevertheless, there are moments when it becomes so cloudy or foggy that you need to cleanse it. If you don't, it will not perform its best and consequently lead to spiritual imbalances manifested into your life. Instant aura cleansing is quite simple and easy to complete on your own, even though supervision is required for those of you who are new to this spiritual experience.

What you can do is stand up comfortably and close your eyes. Visualize that your heart is opening up like a flower blooming. Request that you are bathed in divine light and love, calling on your archangels and spiritual guides. Ask that your aura is thoroughly cleansed, shielding your powerful energy. After finishing with your requests, visualize a pure golden light from the divine right on top of your head. This is the source of light shining bright above you, having traveled through the Great Central Sun into our own dimensions and existence.

The light will slowly come down on you, following the shape of your body and filling you with divine energy. Feel this light going through your entire body, from head to toes. It will then be absorbed by the ground, shaping a platform of light below you. A second golden orb of light will then come and lower itself, bathing you once more with its divine nature. This time, it will remain in your abdominal area.

Visualize that it stays there, as you are breathing in and expanding it with every breath. Your vibration is elevated, as this light is purifying your aura and balancing your spirit.

A third light moves towards your Heart chakra, where it rests and fills your heart with pure bright light. The light is illuminating your aura, expanding in every direction. Once again, another golden orb of light is concentrated around your head and illuminates your third eye. These three distinct energy centers that have been formed in your abdomen, your heart and your mind are perfectly aligned with the deep energy center of the earth's core, as well as the ultimate energy source of the Great Central Sun. This creates a steady pillar of energy flowing through you, cleansing your aura and removing anything toxic.

You can repeat the same visualization as frequently as you like. It will always help you to get grounded and attune to your divine nature. As you become more familiar with the spiritual world, you will be able to achieve even greater connection, activating your energy centers and allowing yourself to shine.

Chapter 10: Amazing Guided Meditations to Banish Negative Entities, Cleanse Your Aura and Supercharge Your Life

By now, you are well aware of the amazing benefits deriving from clearing any negative energy from your body and your home. Now you are ready to continue with guided meditation, in order to experience the wonderful results. Get in a receptive state, ask for help from your spiritual guides and be prepared for the gorgeous changes lying ahead. Through these easy-to-follow guided meditations, you will be able to channel your energy and request the things you seek most in your life. Do you want to clear the atmosphere in your home or at the office? Do you wish to confront a traumatic experience from a past life that has caused you to get stuck in an endless loop?

You have the power to request help from the archangels, reaching out to your divine spirit. They are here to protect you, offering their support and guiding you through the most difficult times. Whether you want to banish an evil spirit, motivate an earthbound entity to pass on to another space, attract abundance or cleanse your electromagnetic field, meditations are a powerful ally of yours. They help you concentrate on your intentions, express them firmly and with absolute clarity.

Below you will see 5 different guided meditations for you to try out. Some of them are simple, whereas others require the presence of the angels to guide you. Depending on your needs and desires, you can choose the meditation that ticks all the boxes for you, allowing you to shine.

Home Protection Meditation with Crystals

This guided meditation will help you protect your home from any negative entities, purify the atmosphere and attract positivity, feeling safe and secure. It will allow you to get rid of unwanted energies that mess with your balance, restoring your inner peace and serenity. For this meditation, you are going to need 4 white candles, 4 black gemstones (black tourmaline, black obsidian and onyx) and eight clear quartz crystals. You can omit the last part, although it amplifies the benefits you get out of the entire protective session. If you want, you can burn sage for a complete reset of your energies.

Place one candle in front of you, one at the back and one on each side of yours. Light the candles and place the black gemstones in between them. If you also have the crystals, you can place each one by the candles and the gemstones. Light the sage and let it burn safely. You have created a circle of light and therefore you need to sit comfortably in the center of this circle.

After having completed the setup of your room, you are now ready to begin your meditation. Close your eyes and focus on your breathing. Take deep breaths slowly, until you feel completely relaxed. Breathe slowly, effortlessly. Focus on the area surrounding your body, becoming aware of your weight. Picture that you are sitting on top of the earth, connecting to its energy in its entirety. The earth is supporting and protecting you throughout this session. The black gemstones have great protective powers and they will join forces, so that you remain safe and secure in this ritual.

Imagine the earth's energy springing from its depths and flooding you with light. This light is cleansing your aura, as it shines through you and removes any negative energy. Through its powerful energy, this light dissolves any negative entities that have been undermining your safety. You can sigh with relief, as you are protected by the archaic energy field of the earth. Gradually, a bubble is created around you. This is your protective shield. No ill wishes, no attachments, no malevolent gazes can get to you, as you are armored with this impenetrable bubble.

This bubble has sprung from within you, filling with the pure white light emerging from the depths of the earth. After a while, the bubble expands and reaches the walls of your room. It has become larger, so that it removes any negative energies. As you are cleansing the space around you with the bubble that is filled with bright purifying light, concentrate on the points of entry within your home. The windows and doors are enhanced, in order to provide an extra feeling of security.

Having completed the protection of your home up to this point, it is now time for the bubble to expand one last time. It becomes bigger and bigger, until it covers your whole home. Let it fill with bright light from the energy of the earth, so as to cleanse everything around you. You are completely protected by the divine nature of the earth. When you have secured everything, you can start focusing on your breathing again. Slowly breathe in and out, inhale through the nose and exhale through the mouth. Open your eyes and resume consciousness.

This meditation enables you to reinforce the protection of your home and by repeating often you can enhance its effectiveness. Do that and enjoy the safety of your dearest place on earth.

Meditation for Clear Negative Energy within Your Home

Your home is your shelter and you need to feel good when you are in it. This is non-negotiable. Unfortunately, there are times when these feelings of security, positive thinking and happiness are disrupted by stagnant energies and malevolent entities. It is therefore imperative that you perform targeted rituals to clear negative energy and purify your home.

Seat comfortably in your room, close your eyes and get into a receptive state. Connect to the energy of your home, in order to request that you change it and remove any negativity. Breathe deeply, as you are connecting to the surrounding energies. There is a lot of residual energy within your home, as it has been piling up for a long time. Request your spiritual guide or the angels that have been looking out for you to help cleanse the negative energy. Start with the room, where you spend most of your time. Visualize the conflict of the energy that has been stuck in this room.

As that energy has been built up over time, it has solidified. So by getting in the room, you get adapted to that particular energy. This can be destructive for your higher purpose. Choose to clear the atmosphere and dissolve the negativity from every corner. Do not forget to breathe deeply, releasing the tension throughout this energy cleaning session. Ask that any negativity is removed from your home. it is equally important to clear the energy from every single item of your home. Visualize that the bad vibes from through these items, leaving your home for good. Let the negative energy escape your room, go through the kitchen, up the staircases and eventually leave the house from an entry point. This is a cathartic procedure, so give this time.

When you are done, open your eyes and take some moments to relax and regain your consciousness. You will be amazed at the results you see at home. No more oppressed, heavy atmosphere. Instead, you will be glad to enter a safe haven, filled with lightness and positive vibes.

Aura Cleansing Meditation

By using the violet flame, this guided meditation is meant to help you cleanse your aura deeply. Restore your electromagnetic vibrational balance, lifting your spirit and clearing out any negative energies that conflict with your positive presence.

Close your eyes. Take a deep breath, and notice how you calm down more with each breath. Feel relaxed, as you let go of the tension. Breathe in through your nose, exhaling gently from the mouth. Visualize a violet light coming down from the sky on the top of your head. This bright light sits on your Crown chakra. Observe the light and every detail. Feel the energy, as it runs through your body. Imagine yourself bathed in that precious, divine light. Visualize your face, as you are smiling blissfully.

The powerful light melts away any negative entities, any stagnant energies within your body. This violet light transforms any negativity, absorbing it completely. Call upon your guardian angels and protectors to help you become more serene, dissolving negative spirits and maintaining your inner balance. Request that this abundant violent light shines upon your aura, sealing it against any threat. Visualize your aura getting fortified by the light.

Hold on to that feeling of knowing that you are thoroughly protected against any negative energy or malevolence trying to harm you. This is a precious feeling of utter joy and satisfaction. The violet light that has come from above offered you this feeling generously. Experience happiness and don't let go of that feeling. Instead, expand it all around your body.

Meditate in silence, as you are contemplating this wonderful experience of protection and aura cleansing. You have been blessed with the purification of your aura and you feel wonderful about it. Breathe in and out slowly, gently, effortlessly. Be present in the moment, without any distractions or obstacles getting in the way. You are happy, utterly and completely joyful.

When you feel good about yourself, open your eyes and slowly regain consciousness. Continue breathing deeply, remembering how wonderful that experience was. You feel lighter than ever before. More than that, you feel illuminated. Stretch your body and feel the calmness all around you. You are revived, filled with energy and pleasure.

Remember to repeat the same ritual every time you feel like you lack energy and liveliness. Since your aura is not static, it fluctuates in size and so you need to make sure that you take care of it.

Meditation with the Angels for Clearing Negative Energy

The angels can be of paramount assistance to you, in your endeavor to release any negativity from your body or your surroundings. It is important that you maintain your calmness throughout this guided meditation. Release any bad vibe, allowing yourself to sigh with relief at the thought of having dissolved negative energies all around.

Close your eyes, breathe in and out gently and feel your body relax with every breath. Focus on your intentions and firmly request assistance from your guardian angels: *"Archangel Michael, archangel Raphael, I seek your presence here. I want you to come and support me in my effort to remove negative energies and restore goodness."* Suddenly, you will start feeling their presence nearby. They will come to help you, protecting you against all harm.

Relax even further and visualize a pure white light. The light shines bright all the way from the sky to your crown, on top of your head. It enters your body through the Crown chakra and runs smoothly through all the energy centers until your feet. The light flows through you and reaches your aura, cleansing it and filling it with positive high vibrational frequencies. Eventually, the light passes through you and connects to the very center of the earth. This is the divine energy in perfect alignment.

Since this divine pure light has shone through you, you need to draw your attention to your inner self. You will see a light shining brighter than ever before from within you. This light is connected to your life force, becoming stronger every single moment. The archangels are standing very close to you. They protect you during this process. So feel this inner power of yours glowing and expanding. Repeat positive affirmations about your enlightenment: *"I am a powerful human being, filled with divine light."*

You are in charge of the energies that flow through you. It is in your power to choose which energies to allow and which ones to reject. No one else has that power over you. This is something you need to believe in, as you are visualizing your omnipotence.

Now archangel Raphael comes closer, healing you and your energy. You feel the comfort from this experience, repeating the following: *"I reject any negative connection that does not serve my higher purpose in life. I command that any negative energies leave my body, never to return again. I stand only in the light and love of my Creator."*

Open your eyes, breathe in and out slowly and take a few moments to resume your consciousness. This is an intense meditation, which requires the divine protection of the archangels. After that, you will feel more confident, loving of yourself and independent.

Guided Meditation to Heal Past Trauma

Past lives can affect you in many ways. If you have been stuck in a problematic situation, unable to move forward, then it is essential that you revisit your past lives and figure out how to push through. Sometimes you need to heal a traumatic experience from another life, before being able to move forward with your current one.

Close your eyes and think of a place where you seem to come back to again and again. This can be a loop from a different lifetime, representing an experience that has made you stuck. Breathe in through your nose and out through your mouth. Relax and let go of your concerns, your thoughts, your traumas. Feel the energy into your soul get in your physical body, as you are exhaling gently. This process makes you feel grounded, aware of the slightest part of your body.

Even though you will remain in your physical body, your thoughts will wander along with your soul. Through your mind, you will have the chance to envision everything absolutely clearly, under the guidance and constant protection of your angels. You will gradually feel your body getting heavier. Now, focus on your third eye. Breathe deeply, as you are feeling your Crown and Third Eye chakras open up. Drift into the past. Be open-minded to what you are about to discover.

You will notice energies that are floating. Request that they show you where you have been stuck, so that you can release yourself from this ongoing ordeal. You need to move forward in your current lifetime. As you delve deeper, you will see images of your past lives run before your eyes. Embrace them without judgment. This is a very delicate procedure, until you manage to envision the experience that has caused your trauma.

As soon as you discover this traumatic experience, you need to gather details about it by settling more comfortably. What year is it? In which country are you located? What language are you speaking? Take a look around you and observe every little detail. Remind yourself that you are just an observer and therefore you don't have to be afraid.

Watch your trauma as it unfolds, knowing that you are safe at all times. Process what has happened, breathing deeply and remaining calm throughout the entire experience. After having observed everything clearly, you need to express your gratitude. Say *"thank you"* for the important lesson that this experience has given to you. Acknowledge that it had to happen, so that you could evolve in your next lives. Forgive, love and remember. Release negative energy with every exhale.

Now it is time to get back to your physical body. Feel the protective presence of the archangels, holding your hand throughout your travel and until you have settled to your physical presence. Inhale and exhale deeply, feeling your spirit extremely lighter than before. Bring your thoughts to the present moment, revaluating the situation that had been causing you discomfort.

Chapter 11: The 7 Day Negative Energy Cleanse Ritual to Enchant Your Home with Angelic Power

What does it take for you to call on your guardian angels for help? How can you request their presence and seek their unconditional support in your endeavors? It is true that angels are always by your side, even if you cannot see them. More often than not, we get to feel their presence around us. We are sure that they are right by our side every step of the way, no matter how long it takes for us to stop needing them.

Our connection with the angels is profoundly spiritual. It enables us to communicate with the divine and feel safe in a world filled with dangers lurking in every corner. It is a dangerous place we live in, but our spiritual guides are always here to lay a helping hand and offer their wisdom. This is how we pull through, get it together and survive any hardships that emerge along the way.

After having analyzed several different aspects of clearing the energy within your home and your body, the only thing that's missing is a practical approach for your everyday life. I know that I have promised you in the title that you can get tangible results for spiritual cleansing in just 7 days. In fact, you will see that a week is more than enough, if you follow my guidelines below.

The daily ritual secret formula that I have designed for you is able to reset the energy within your home. You will not need to spend your entire day trying different time-consuming rituals for removing all bad vibes from your personal sanctuary. On the contrary, these steps that I have included within the formula are easy to implement in your daily routine. They are also fun and you will most likely end up sticking with these morning habits, even after the completion of your experimental week.

Be open-minded about this week. Wake up with an optimistic feeling, a sensation that everything is going to be alright. In this way, you are going to attract these positive vibes and cast away any negative thoughts trying to creep into your mind. The Law of Attraction works and therefore you should follow its principles to skyrocket your potential in life. You must keep the faith, as this is a helpful asset in your attempt to improve your life on so many different levels.

Even if you get bored or lack the will to perform your morning ritual, you are advised not to slip up. You need to be consistent, so as to provide optimum results in the end. If you sleep in and wake up later than usual, make the necessary adjustments, in order to fit this ritual into your busy schedule. Do not postpone or delay or cancel your energy cleansing. If you do, you will soon realize that negative entities are far more persistent—After all, perseverance is often the key to success.

Negative Energy Cleansing Daily Ritual Secret Formula

As you are reaching the end of this book, it is essential that you have all the tools you are going to need towards clearing negative energy and malevolent spirits from your home. Below, you can see a secret formula you can use as a daily ritual. This will help you purify your home in as little as 7 days. Be consistent and detailed when performing this ritual. It consists of simple things that you can easily do on a daily basis. The ritual is fast, requiring no more than 30 minutes of your time. Wake up in the morning, open the windows to let the fresh air in and allow the sun to flood the room. Wear your widest smile and start your day with the following secret formula.

Step 1: Express Your Gratitude

Start your day every morning, by expressing what you are grateful for in your life. Is it your family, a newborn kid that has added to your happiness, or maybe your career? Be extremely detailed when you are saying *"thank you"* for specific things in life you have received. Rather than say *"thank you for my work,"* you can just as easily say *"thank you for the wonderful opportunity I have been given at work to collaborate with one of the best associates in the company."* The former statement is too generic, whereas the latter fills you with a higher vibrational frequency right away.

This step should take around 5 minutes. You can keep a journal if you want. Otherwise, simply close your eyes and meditate. Express your gratitude out loud, channeling it to the things that bring you joy and make you feel satisfied. As soon as you start doing that, you will instantly feel better. You will realize how much you already have, which is always a great reminder in case you have taken that for granted. Being conscious of what you have accomplished is amazing, as it boosts your self-confidence and makes you feel good about yourself.

Step 2: Practice EFT Tapping

You are now ready to move forward to the next step and raise your vibration. One of the coolest ways to do so is by practicing EFT tapping. Concentrate on your head and the area of the neck, the chest and armpits for this quick, yet effective tapping session. It doesn't have to be anything elaborate. You just begin tapping the external part of your palm, as you are repeating positive affirmations about yourself. You can say that you are awesome, you are a great worker, you are devoted to your goals or you are an extrovert. Whatever makes your heart beat faster, you should express it through these affirmations.

By tapping on the forehead, your third eye right between your eyebrows, the area under your eyes and your cheekbones, your upper lip and chin, you can continue repeating those amazing affirmations. They will make you feel much better, by elevating your vibrational frequencies even further. Tapping creates vibrations that are beneficial to your well-being. When combined with verbal stimulants that promote joy and satisfaction, the result is even more impressive. Typically, an EFT tapping session will take you about 10 minutes.

Step 3: Use Essential Oils

What a better way to start your day than with the intoxicating fragrances of essential oils! I have referred earlier in this book to the powerful healing properties of lemongrass. However, you can try out different essential oils that clear negative energy and boost your mood. Just use an essential oil diffuser to spread the aromas all over the place. In fact, you can combine that with drinking a warm cup of herbal tea or chamomile. This will give you the chance to hydrate, soothe your soul and wake up naturally.

Some of the best essential oils to use besides lemongrass include peppermint, sweet orange, rosemary, cypress and juniper berry. Along with the use of essential oils, you can also burn Palo Santo wood. It smells amazing, cleansing the atmosphere from any negative energies piling up in the room. If you have the items at hand, this step will require 10 minutes of your time along with the preparation of your liquid bliss to sip on.

Step 4: Visualizations

You have already heightened your vibrational frequencies, so you must be feeling over the moon. In order to make the most of your morning ritual, you should not forget to include visualizations in the mix. These visualizations will offer you the opportunity to manifest exactly what you want to attract in your life, so that they are drawn by your energy. This is a lovely way to increase your vibration, while at the same time experiencing your desires right now. Instead of projecting your desire into the future, you live as if you have already acquired what you are looking for.

By visualizing that you are accomplished, happy, abundant and successful, healthy and outgoing, you experience the emotions flowing through these states. How would you feel if you were successful in your profession? Try to visualize that and see what it means for you, emotionally-wise. Again, this step usually requires 5 minutes to complete.

Step 5: Tidy Your Room

I am sure you are well aware of the significance of a tidied place by now. After completing these 4 steps that have filled you with joy and have skyrocketed your energy from within, it is important to tidy up your room a little. Of course, I am not talking about dusting or vacuuming. These chores can be parts of a deeper cleaning that takes place once a week or so. I am referring to the powerful effects of making your bed and cleaning your workspace, your armchair, your bedside table and anything else you keep within reach.

By doing so, you remain grounded and you feel accomplished about having done something meaningful so early on in your day. Making your bed is an excellent way to remain disciplined, organized and in line with your inner balance. No more than 5 minutes will be enough, assuming that you keep everything in place.

Step 5+1: Use Your DIY Spray

To wrap things up with your morning ritual, take a moment and use your powerful DIY spray to remove negative energy. This spray contains rose petals, which are extremely high in vibrational frequencies. It also contains sage, which is a potent purifier and cleanser of energy. Along with water, these wonderful ingredients create a secret formula that works wonders for your personal space.

Just spray the cleansing spray and rinse. This can be used daily and you can even spray it on yourself, as it contains no chemicals or preservatives. It is 100% natural and organic, offering a great option for cleaning and removing any negativity. Once more, you will need 5 minutes to complete this step.

Tips for the Best Daily Ritual

You should adhere to the morning ritual I have laid out for you for at least 7 days. During this time, you will certainly notice a remarkable change in the energy of your home. In fact, the negative energies will disappear and in their place you will feel the lightness of positivity. Your sleep will improve and you will have no issues bothering you for no actual reason.

After a week has passed, you are free to continue with this ritual on a daily basis. If you do, you will see that things are only getting better. Incorporate some of the guided meditations I have created for you and you will never have to deal with such negative energies again in your life.

If you want to enhance the power of your visualizations, you can also use crystals and gemstones. Black obsidian, onyx and black tourmaline are exquisite for clearing the negative energy, as you know. A wide range of precious stones and crystals can be found in the market, ready to help you reach your goals much faster. In addition, you can experiment with several other healing items. Scented candles, Tibetan singing bowls, amulets and talismans, are all going to boost your own powers and take you higher.

A Nighttime Ritual to Cleanse Your Energy

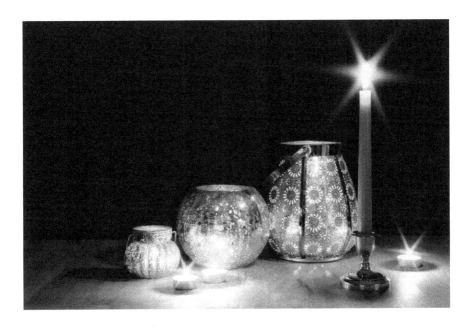

You have spent an entire day on the go, performing your scheduled tasks and mingling with a lot of people. Now the time has come for you to return home, in the comfort of your personal shelter. You are in your safe haven and you want nothing more than to relax, letting go of the tension and enjoying precious moments alone, or with those you hold dear to you.

First of all, it is good that you take a soothing shower before going to bed. I am guessing not many people can indulge in a bath with salts and essential oils every single night. However, you can have a warm shower and use products that help you relax. Let the water run through your skin and remove any toxic thought, along with dead skin cells and dust. Let go of the evil eye, as well as any other negative energy that has been accumulated on your body.

As soon as you finish showering, you should rinse your skin with a soft towel and begin your beauty routine. Do whatever makes you happy; use a scrub to exfoliate your skin, apply moisturizing cream to hydrate your body and comb your hair. When you get into the bedroom, make sure that you have created a welcoming, relaxing atmosphere. Play some soothing, inspirational music in the background. You can use mantras, if you want. Otherwise, any relaxing music will do.

Light a candle or two. Dim the lights or use the candlelight as your sole source of brightness within the room. Burn incense with your favorite fragrances. I would suggest using camphor, as it allows you to clear the negative energy and rejuvenate. Concentrate on your breathing and meditate for a few moments. Close your eyes, listening to the sounds of the mantras or relaxing music in the distance. Picture a bright light on the crown of your head, slowly moving downwards and filling you with its overwhelming power.

Experience this moment of pure bright light filling you from within, flooding every organ, every part of your body, every cell. Visualize the light expanding and reaching your aura. Feel your aura as it gets purified, utterly cleansed by the divine light. This visualization helps you align your energy centers, creating a connection between the grounded energy of the earth and the mystical energy of the divine. With that in mind, keep breathing deeply and concentrate on the present.

Finish your visualization with a wide smile on your face. Avoid any artificial light and steer clear from any electronic device for at least an hour before bedtime. Once you lie down, close your eyes and manifest your desires. Have those positive thoughts in your mind, as you are drifting away in the sweetest dreams. You will be enjoying a restful night, having cleared the negative energies within your room and having balanced your inner energy. Good night!

Conclusion

You have successfully reached the final chapter of my book. I hope that you have found it helpful, in your attempt to interpret the spiritual world and delve into the mysteries of the divine. It is amazing what you can do in your life, simply by aligning your energy with the energy of the cosmos. By now you have discovered what it feels like to be cursed or the victim of the evil eye and you have learned how to cleanse your aura and energy chakras.

Furthermore, you have read through guided meditations that allow you to practice what you have been taught theoretically about negative energies, unwanted guests and entities from a different world. This has been a wonderful journey in the mystical philosophies of the world, dictating that you need to find the balance from within yourself, before you are able to thrive in your life. First, you have to cleanse your own body and soul, before you move on to the next level and purify your direct environment.

There are evil entities out there, wanting to do you harm. However, this should not bring you down or lead you to despair. Besides, you are not alone in this world. You have a network of family members, friends and of course your spiritual guides to help you out in times of need. This book has hopefully inspired you to further elaborate on spirituality and the mysteries lying beneath the surface. It would be great if you followed up with more information about several other parts of the divine world.

Introduce healthy practices in your life, such as performing meditations, yoga and Pilates, EFT tapping, TRE and Reiki. All these techniques aim at boosting your vibration to make you healthier and happier in your life. Isn't this what you have been searching for? If you could accomplish that in an all-natural, non-invasive manner, then it would make no sense to reject such an offer. There are methods that have been conceived out of pure necessity. These methods have been proven extremely useful when dealing with the spiritual world.

Another piece of advice from me would be to join communities of like-minded people. In this way, you will be able to discuss the things that matter to you the most. They will understand you, offering their own wisdom and practical information that might end up saving your life. You should not be afraid to express your needs and desires. Find the right people to surround you, so as to feel comfortable talking about what is troubling you. Communication is a key element in forming healthy relationships, after all.

Looking back at the time when I wrote *"Spiritual Cleansing: Soul Cleansing Secrets No One Talks About & How To*

Cleanse Negative Energy From Your House In 7 Days (Positive Energy For Home)," I feel grateful and happy. It is my honor to be able and share my hard-earned knowledge on the subject. Through my experiments with different approaches, I have read thousands of books and I have spoken to thousands of people. What I have obtained from every single one of them is literally invaluable.

Now that you have read through my book, I hope that we meet again soon. I am wishing you love, light and courage on your journey. By taking initiative and getting all the way through this book, you have completed the most difficult part of the entire process. This was a fantastic idea and you have so many wonderful things to look forward to now that you have read all about it!

References

andreas160578. (2016a). *Salt Spa Wellness.* https://pixabay.com/photos/salt-spa-wellness-wood-1884166/

Anthony, K. (2017, December). *EFT Tapping.* Healthline; Healthline Media. https://www.healthline.com/health/eft-tapping

Bejan, A., & Lorente, S. (2010). The constructal law of design and evolution in nature. *Philosophical Transactions of the Royal Society B: Biological Sciences, 365*(1545), 1335–1347. https://doi.org/10.1098/rstb.2009.0302

Bledsoe, D. A. (2013, October 1). *The Evil Eye: Ancient, Yet Contemporary Phenomenon and a Biblical Response.* Missionexus.org. https://missionexus.org/the-evil-eye-ancient-yet-contemporary-phenomenon-and-a-biblical-response/

Camille Noe Pagán. (2018, January 11). *What Is Aromatherapy?* WebMD; WebMD. https://www.webmd.com/balance/stress-management/aromatherapy-overview#1

Collins, N. (2016, July 14). *Science Says Burning Sage Can Clean The Air And Improve Your Health.* Lifehack. https://www.lifehack.org/426156/science-says-burning-sage-can-clean-the-air-and-improve-your-health

Corbin, K. (n.d.). *The Law of Attraction and Quantum Physics – Law of Attraction Resource Guide.* Https://

Www.Lawofattractionresourceguide.com/. https://www.lawofattractionresourceguide.com/the-law-of-attraction-and-quantum-physics/

dhandapani, basker. (2017). Angel Woman White. https://pixabay.com/photos/angel-woman-white-girl-young-2816236/

Fiona, K. (2017). *Buddha Relax Relaxation*. https://pixabay.com/photos/buddha-relax-relaxation-asia-2109894/

freeAgent42, T. K. @. (2018, October 22). *"The field is the sole governing agency of the particle" Einstein*. Medium. https://medium.com/@tonyknight_92437/the-field-is-the-sole-governing-agency-of-the-particle-einstein-1f770090a926

Glady. (2013). *Rose Flower Dew*. https://pixabay.com/photos/rose-flower-dew-dewdrops-droplets-165819/

hassan, mohamed. (2018). *Meditation Zen Chan*. https://pixabay.com/photos/meditation-zen-chan-yoga-statue-3338691/

ImagesBG. (2017a). *Meditation Nature Yoga*. https://pixabay.com/photos/meditation-nature-yoga-sun-clouds-2001317/

Lolame. (2018). *Candles Still Life*. https://pixabay.com/photos/candles-still-life-candlestick-3493575/

M, R. (2019). An Overview of the Thymus. EndocrineWeb. https://www.endocrineweb.com/endocrinology/overview-thymus

Mannonen, T. (2016). Crystals Stones Healing Mystic. https://pixabay.com/photos/crystals-stones-healing-mystic-1567953/

Markus1308. (2020). *Bank Nature Bench.* https://pixabay.com/photos/bank-nature-bench-rest-loneliness-5103277/

McCutcheon, S. (2018). Positive Thinking Energy. https://pixabay.com/photos/positive-thinking-energy-reiki-3805169/

monicore. (2016b). Essential Oils Aromatherapy. https://pixabay.com/photos/essential-oils-aromatherapy-spa-oil-1433694/

Pexels. (2016c). *Alternative Energy Aura.* https://pixabay.com/photos/alternative-energy-aura-energetic-1869248/

Pexels. (2016). Meditate Meditation Peaceful. https://pixabay.com/photos/meditate-meditation-peaceful-1851165/

Photo, D. (2017). Self Confidence Force Woman. https://pixabay.com/photos/self-confidence-force-wave-sea-2036236/

Photos, F. (2015). *Sunset Dusk Silhouette.* https://pixabay.com/photos/sunset-dusk-silhouette-shadow-girl-691848/

Pitkanen, M. (2018, June). *(PDF) The experiments of Masaru Emoto with emotional imprinting of water.* ResearchGate. https://www.researchgate.net/publication/

335909571_The_experiments_of_Masaru_Emoto_w ith_emotional_imprinting_of_water

piro4d. (2016b). *Feng Shui Zen Stones*. https:// pixabay.com/photos/feng-shui-zen-stones-texture-1927590/

sorcel. (2014). Amulet Evil Eyes. https://pixabay.com/ photos/amulet-evil-eyes-turkey-blue-charm-458235/

StockSnap. (2017). *People Woman Happy*. https:// pixabay.com/photos/people-woman-happy-relax-travel-2588546/

vetsikas1969, dimitris. (2020). *Girl Meditation Nature*. https://pixabay.com/photos/girl-meditation-nature-yoga-4981766/

Voicu, A. (2016). Woman Beauty Wreath. https:// pixabay.com/photos/woman-beauty-wreath-fashion-1403458/

Wikipedia Contributors. (2019, May 8). Atlas (mythology). Wikipedia; Wikimedia Foundation. https:// en.wikipedia.org/wiki/Atlas_(mythology)

Get Your *BONUS* FREE Manifesting Secret Formula Toolkit!

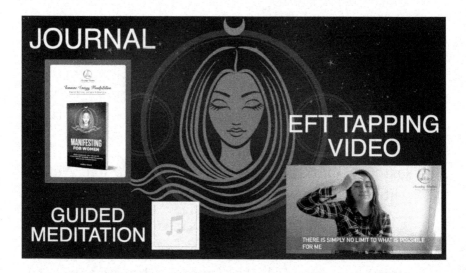

Are you DONE with settling for a mediocre life, wasting precious time, & ready to live your wildest fantasies?

- Hack your brain, boost performance, & release blocks holding you back from greatness

- Awaken this amazing energy to supercharge your manifestations

- Stop wasting what little precious time you have on ineffective methods

Manifesting Secret Formula Toolkit Includes:

1. **Supercharged Manifestation EFT Tapping Video** Download To Banish Limiting Beliefs & Propel You Toward Your Dream Life! (Infused with 432 Hz Frequency)

2. **Secret Formula Journal!** Daily manifestation Ritual Done For You, Simply Rinse & Repeat At Home! (You Can Print This Out, Stick On Your Wall, & Cross Off The Days You Complete The Ritual)

3. **Powerful 10 Minute 'Shifting Your reality' Guided Meditation** MP3 Download (Infused with 528 Hz Frequency)

4. ***BONUS*** LOA boosting 10 Minute 'Feminine Energy Awakening' Guided Meditation MP3 Download

Click Here to Get Your *BONUS* FREE Manifesting Secret Formula Toolkit!:

bit.ly/manifestingforwomen

Please Leave a Review on Amazon

From the bottom of my heart, thank you for reading my book. I truly hope that it helps you on your spiritual journey and to live a more empowered and happy life. If it does help you, then I'd like to ask you for a favor. Would you be kind enough to leave an honest review for this book on Amazon? It'd be greatly appreciated and will likely impact the lives of other spiritual seekers across the globe, giving them hope and power. I read **every** review I receive and they help me to become the best writer and spiritual teacher that I can be.

Thank you and good luck!

Angela Grace

Why not join our Facebook community and discuss your spiritual path with like-minded seekers?

We would love to hear from you!

Click here to join the 'Ascending Vibrations' community:

bit.ly/ascendingvibrations